SO-CPD-447

WELCOME to the MOTHERHOOD

Grime and Punishment

Melissa Jarvis

MEDFORD

PRESS

Plexus Publishing
Medford, New Jersey

First printing, 2004

Welcome to the Motherhood: Grime and Punishment

Copyright © 2004 by Melissa Jarvis

A Medford Press Book, published by:
Plexus Publishing, Inc.
143 Old Marlton Pike
Medford, New Jersey 08055
U.S.A.

All rights reserved. No part of this book may be reproduced in any form or by any electronic or mechanical means, including information storage and retrieval systems, without permission in writing from the publisher, except by a reviewer, who may quote brief passages in a review.

"Boy Feet" and "Dr. Doom" are reprinted herein with the permission of *The Courier-Post*, for which they were originally written as an installment of Melissa Jarvis's weekly column, "Family Album." ©2001 *The Courier-Post*. Some other chapters include or are based upon stories that first appeared in "Family Album" but have been significantly revised and expanded by the author.

Library of Congress Cataloging-in-Publication Data
Jarvis, Melissa, 1965–
    Welcome to the motherhood : grime and punishment / Melissa Jarvis.
        p. cm.
    ISBN 0-9666748-4-7 (pbk.)
    1. Motherhood--Humor. 2. Child rearing--Humor. 3. Home economics--Humor. I. Title.
    PN 6231.M68J37 2004
        814'.6--dc22
                                                                    2004008137

Printed and bound in The United States of America

Publisher: Thomas H. Hogan, Sr.
Editor-in-Chief: John B. Bryans
Managing Editor: Deborah R. Poulson
Graphics Department Director: M. Heide Dengler
Sales Manager: Pat Palatucci
Copy Editor: Pat Hadley-Miller
Book Designer: Kara Mia Jalkowski
Cover Designer: Erica Pannella

Back cover photo by David Michael Howarth

For more information about books from Plexus Publishing, Inc., call (609) 654-6500 or visit our Web site at www.plexuspublishing.com

Dedication

To My Father, Donald E. Hough—Writer, Artist, engineer, softball coach, and so much more, who passed away during the writing of this book, and who definitely would have thought it was neat that one of us landed a book deal. I miss you.

And to my best friend and handsome husband, Mike, who helped produce so much of the material inside. I go to bed every night feeling like the luckiest woman in the world.

Contents

Acknowledgments

THIS BOOK COULDN'T HAVE BEEN WRITTEN WERE IT NOT FOR the incredible people in my life who are there for me on a daily basis. The women of my little town, sometimes referred to as "Springers," make me so proud to be one of them. Some juggle kids on their hips while others juggle careers, but they are all fascinating to observe from my writer's perspective. These ordinary neighborhood moms who love what they do and do it so well are the women for whom this book is meant, especially Debbie Chiarulli, who has been a big part of my little world since we were 12 years old. Thank you all for your friendship.

I'd also like to thank my mother, Shirley Hough, who took such loving care of my father during his last months while this book was being written, and my sister and friend, Cindy Caffrey. You've both shown me that it is the love of a family that lends importance to a life.

Thank you also to the Jarvis clan—MJ, Mugsy, Dan, Chris, and Don. Although you made me promise not to write about you, I love you all.

John B. Bryans, Editor in Chief of Plexus Books, is the person who got this whole thing up and running. It doesn't matter how good you are at something in life if somebody doesn't invest his energy in your efforts. Thank you, John, for your invaluable assistance. I can promise you that I'll try to make the most of the wonderful opportunity you have given me.

To all the hard-working people at Plexus Publishing, Inc., including Tom Hogan, Deborah Poulson, Kara Jalkowski, Pat Palatucci, Heide Dengler, and Lisa Wrigley, thank you for believing in me. Until now, my biggest accomplishment was the Little League team back in 1979, when we almost made it to the Little League World Series. Thank goodness you've given me something else to cling to, because my friends tell me that was getting old!

A number of individuals took the time to read early drafts of the manuscript, offering helpful feedback and encouragement as well as input on the book's title. My thanks go to Janet Gramza Marino, Kristin Solem, Lauri Rimler, Sarah Bongey, Mary Rowles, Mark Voight, and Jan King.

I would be remiss if I didn't thank the wonderful people at the *Courier-Post* newspaper for giving me my first break as a writer. Rosemary Parillo, thank you for telling me all those years ago that I should really write a book. I hope you like it. And to my fans from around South Jersey who write to me each week, your words always inspire me. Thank you.

Acknowledgments

To Dan Ward, you are a true friend and a mentor. We are so lucky to have you and Lisa as our neighbors. Thank you both.

Life is always happier when we're in the company of our wonderful friends, Jake and Linda Fleischer. Our days playing softball in South Philly will stay with me forever. How nice that you are part of our children's memories as well. Thank you both for bringing such love and joy to our family.

And finally, to the gang at the dinner table each night, who refer to me as "the third most famous person we know." That's okay, I don't mind being listed after Master Giacobbe and Jordan's grandmom, who invented Olympic Day at school. Living life as your mom has given me all the joy my heart could ever hold. I love you Sam, McKenna, and Dylan, and I simply adore your daddy.

Introduction:
Out on a Limb

THE WOMAN HUNG UP THE PHONE, A BEMUSED EXPRESSION ON her carefully made up face. She tapped the gleaming kitchen counter with a manicured nail, and then turned quickly to her family waiting anxiously for the news.

"Well everyone, it seems Mommy will be writing a book!" She was immediately surrounded with tight hugs and cheers of happiness. Overcome with emotion, she found a free hand and dabbed at her eyes with a handkerchief. Life was good indeed.

That's how things happen in books. Other books. Certainly not this one. This book is about real people, stuck together in real families, living real lives.

Real moms know that whenever the phone rings, there's a high-pitched whistle that blows, which is only heard by those under the age of 12. At that precise moment, kids drop what they're doing, and one of three things will happen:

They will spontaneously bleed, vomit, or cry or cause a sibling to bleed, vomit, or cry.

Any liquid within a two-mile range of their flailing arms will be spilled.

They will suddenly yearn to know the answers to where babies come from and/or how old one must be before developing nose hair.

Personally, I've rarely looked bemused. The only time I may have approached bemusement is the evening I discovered that my son had painted the inside of the toilet bowl with my nail polish.

So, when I was presented with the opportunity to write a book, I did what any mother who realized she'd now be working full-time from home would do—I panicked.

My unmanicured nails gripped the sides of the phone until my knuckles were white.

Here's the rest of what really happened.

I hung up the phone, and instantly saw a running neon script (the kind I've seen in pictures of Times Square) flashing before my eyes. Squinting, I could just make out the hot-pink words reading, "What, are you kidding yourself? You spend all your time wiping short little people. There's no time to write a book! You bathe with Barbie heads floating in the tub. Last night you mentally balanced your checkbook while fooling around with your husband. You got so tired Saturday night that you watched *Poltergeist* in Spanish because you couldn't work up the energy to find the channel changer. And have you even thought about public appearances? They're out, my friend. You haven't had a real haircut since getting talked into a "Dorothy Hamill" wedge in 1979. You don't own a slip, and frankly, you don't look good in fluorescent lighting. But, hey, good luck!"

Then the script ran out, and I started to come to my senses.

I looked at my kids sitting at the kitchen table. They were smack in the middle of arguing about why movie critics give two thumbs up for a good review when they have a total of four thumbs to use. I half-listened to the merits of their argument as I watched my husband track mud through the kitchen with his work boots. The cat was in the corner, coughing up a hairball, and one of the dogs was at the back door scratching to come in—presumably so it could pee where it preferred: on the new carpet in our bedroom.

In that second I knew. I might have to shove my little darlings under the sofa for nine months to do it, but, by God, I was going to write this book.

I would write it for every woman who ever watched a Martha Stewart special and realized that some parents don't make their kids wear an old suit and go as Jehovah's Witnesses for Halloween. I would write it for every woman whose son asked her loudly in the supermarket if she could make him "vagina" for dinner, when he really meant "lasagna." I would write it for every woman who volunteered for a class trip and got stuck next to "Peter Puker," who really does throw up on school buses. I would write it for every woman whose husband rented *Full Metal Jacket* as a romantic Valentine's night surprise. I would write it for every woman who believes her oven meant it when it claimed to be "self-cleaning."

It was time for my family to know the good news.

I cleared my throat. Smiling brightly, I asked for their attention. "I have something important to tell you." A hand stuck up in the air. "Yes, McKenna?" My oldest daughter looked puzzled. "Mommy, why do kamikaze pilots wear helmets?"

A little nerve in my right eye started twitching, and I swallowed hard. "I have no idea, sweetie." I spoke a little louder. "Now please listen, everyone! Mommy wants to have a powwow. You know—a family meeting."

My son jumped up, knocking over his chair. "We're going camping? All right!" I furrowed my brow. My son was giving his twin sister a high five. "Hey mom, I want my own tent. No girls. Oh, and I'll definitely need a new fishing rod." His little sister Dylan interrupted him, whining, "Why does he get a new fishing rod and not me?" Rolling his eyes, as seven-year-old boys tend to do, he answered her. "Because, stupid, you always adopt the bait and make daddy bring it home for the fish tank. You're weird. You don't even eat animal crackers `cause you think it's mean."

Dylan tugged on my shirt. "Then can I make the first fire?" McKenna stepped in front of her. "No way, mom! She's five! Why does she get to make a fire and not me?"

My husband was just looking back and forth at the chaos like a spectator at a tennis match.

I was suddenly exhausted, and momentarily lost my train of thought. Oh, yeah—the book.

"Okay, everybody needs to calm down. We're not going camping. Well, someday, maybe, but that's not the point. A powwow is a family meeting, not a camping trip."

Dylan burst into tears and collapsed with grief onto the floor. McKenna threw her hands on her hips. "We're not going camping?" she said with attitude. "It's not fair! Every one of my friends has gone camping, and all we ever do is go to the stupid beach!"

I looked down at my feet, shaking my head. Where had I gone wrong? Prior to having kids I had held many intelligent conversations with all kinds of people. I valiantly forged ahead.

"Mommy is going to be busy for the next nine months. This family is going to experience some incredible changes, as we grow together … " I was only half done with my motivational talk when chairs were tipped over, high fives were spread among the natives, and they started a football cheer. This joy didn't include my son, however, who screamed, "Oh, now what, like you're going to have another baby to take care of? This is just great, mom! Now how am I gonna get to hockey when dad's not home!" Running from the table, he hit his plate of food with his elbow and it clattered to the floor.

My husband looked at me, perplexed.

"Uh, sweetie? I know you don't mean that you're pregnant, because we made sure that couldn't happen again, right? Unless something awful went wrong with the surgical procedure I had." He shook his head dramatically. "Oh, yeah, it was just a little surgery, sure, but let's not forget the afternoon I had to spend on the couch with that freezing cold ice bag on me ... there are some guys who take weeks recovering from that, and we're not even going to go into the mental anguish ... " I interrupted his train of pitiful surgical recollections before he could break into verse.

"I am not pregnant."

This, at least, stopped the girls in their tracks, mid-fight over whether we'd name the new baby "Britney" or "Dusty."

"Sorry guys. I'm not pregnant, and we're not going camping." I grinned, hoping the excitement would spread to the masses. "That was the publisher on the phone. My book idea is a 'go,' and they are giving me nine months to write it. Isn't that great?" I clapped for myself.

My husband smiled, but before he could congratulate me, the girls interrupted him with their dramatic departure from the kitchen. One of them stomped on my foot on the way out. "You know, if I was pregnant, that could've hurt!" I yelled after them.

Happily enough, within minutes they banded together and plotted my demise. It always makes a mother proud when her kids can occupy themselves with an imaginative game like "get momma."

This was going to be an interesting nine months.

1

Does the Stay-at-Home Mommy Want a Wittle Awwowance?

"Why Are You Worrying About It So Much? I'll Just Give you an allowance each week, that's all. After all, this is what you wanted, right?" My husband didn't, obviously, understand the images that shot through my head at that particular point in time.

The minute he said the word, "allowance," here is the little home movie that was playing for me:

Barefoot and wearing an old maternity top, even though "the baby" was now in school, I am standing in front of my husband as he sits at his imposing desk paying bills. I wait in line behind our five-year-old, who has just received a peck on the forehead and a five-dollar bill for her monthly allowance. I shuffle up to the front of the line as she skips away with big plans on how to spend her loot.

Clutched in my right hand are some cutouts from a magazine, and I nervously brush away sweat dripping off my brow with the other hand. Clearing my throat, it is my turn. I feel faint from the pressure. "Um, thank you for seeing me on such short notice. I know I've fallen a little behind in the housekeeping, and I'm still not sure how all your underwear turned pink in the laundry, but I'll get better, I swear."

Mike sighs and points to the little papers in my hand. "What are those?"

I stammer nervously, "Oh, these are just some things I thought I could buy if you could add maybe a dollar or two more to my allowance. See, I really need snow boots with this nasty weather we've been having, and I found some on sale. With the coupons and the money I've saved from last month's allowance, I just need two more dollars and I'll have enough."

He considers my request as he spreads the pictures of snow boots in front of him. "Why don't you just put socks on over your flip flops? After all, you bought those new flip flops last summer, and you just had to have them, even though they cost almost three dollars."

"Well, because that's not practical. My feet will freeze!"

Rubbing his temples and shuffling some papers on his desk, he grunts and reaches for his wallet. "Fine, but it's coming out of next month's allowance, okay?"

On bended knee, I thank him profusely and wait for the forehead kiss that never comes. With a tear, I walk away, silently

2

cheering at the new snow boots I'll finally be able to buy. What a happy day!

"Mike, I cannot even begin to tell you how many things are wrong with that sentence. I know you mean well, but I do not want an allowance. The very word makes me shudder with horror, if you must know."

He shakes his head. "Well, okay, then, we'll just have to work out something that you're comfortable with. Maybe we won't call it an allowance. I'll just leave money in an envelope in the desk that you can use when you need stuff, okay?"

I narrowed my eyes. There wasn't anything wrong with that, actually. I *was* a new mother of twins. In a few months, a night job was opening up in my paralegal field. In the meantime though, there was no way to make any money to contribute to the monthly bills. Even if I did consider working full time, having two babies in day care would deplete any money I'd make anyway.

I would just have to get used to my new role. I brightened for a second. "Oh, I know what would make me feel better—let's get out those tax returns from the year we were first married when I made more money than you, remember? That was a good year."

He patted me on the forehead. "You're strange, but I love you anyway. I'm sticking twenty bucks in an envelope if you need it."

3

When I thought about it, I wasn't even sure what I wanted the money for. Hadn't I always dreamed of having babies and staying home to enjoy them? Apparently, as a temporary milking machine that bore but a vague resemblance to the independent woman who had walked into that delivery room, I needed something to cling to. You know—to remind me who I really was.

Some nights, I'd put the babies to bed and go through old pocketbooks, gently unfolding the faded receipts from my previous life.

One night, I did something that probably fell under the category of "crazy new mom." Mike was busy working two jobs to support us, and our mortgage was late. With him working so much, I knew my conversational skills were dwindling. Even the dog was bored by my attempts at witty banter. I was starting to question my sanity.

So I did it. I called a late night hot line that promised "adult talk." I have to admit, it was pretty exciting. It had been eons since I had discussed world events. This would be perfect!

After waiting patiently on the line for five or six minutes, a woman came on. "Ooh," she purred. "Are you ready for some adult talk?"

"Yes, and I have my credit card ready just like the commercial says." I was polite despite the late hour; after all, I needed this woman desperately. "What would you like to talk about?"

She moaned a little, and told me my choices. "Well, honey, we can talk about you. We can talk about me. We can even, for an extra $3.99 a minute, talk about you *and* me." She made that odd moaning sound again. She sounded a lot like the dog when we toss him the leftover burrito on Mexican night.

"Hmm. Well, actually, I was hoping we could talk about investment options, and whether you think it will be a bear or a bull market in the new economy. Or, if you'd rather, we could discuss the ethics of cloning." I was kind of hoping she'd pick the first one, but either would be fine by me. I smiled hopefully.

"Listen, %#@, don't @%# around with me again! I don't have time for this @#$*!"

It took about three weeks for the charges to show on my credit card bill. Sitting there looking at that slip of paper, I realized that my attempts at restoring my sanity had just cost me a small fortune.

When Mike came home and saw the bill, he sounded just like the moaning woman I had tried to discuss world events with. I thought about mentioning the coincidence to him, but there are just some things better left unsaid.

2

Rich Is ...

EVENTUALLY, EVERY KID STARTS TO DEVELOP A CONCEPT OF money. It usually starts with the Tooth Fairy.

With my kids' penchant for eating sticky foods, their Tooth Fairy was racking up some pretty impressive frequent-flier miles. It wasn't long before they had a more attractive financial portfolio than their parents.

My son had just earned his first dollar from the Tooth Fairy when he asked me to explain what "rich" meant. I thought hard. This was important, and I didn't want to screw it up. On the one hand, I didn't want my children to grow into materialistic adults and value the wrong things in life. On the other hand, I certainly wanted them to appreciate a hard day's work and what it took to put food on the table each night.

"Well, son," I began. "Rich is when you don't have to split the toilet paper rolls between the upstairs bathroom and the downstairs one, hoping your kids are fast sprinters. Rich is when you have more than one good light bulb that you move from lamp to lamp, depending on where you want to read. Rich is when you require the services of a concierge and a sommelier in the same night. Rich is not laughing when you say the words concierge and sommelier."

I took a deep breath and continued, buoyed by his respectful attention. "Rich is hardcover, not paperback. Rich means never having to wait until it comes out on video. Rich is ordering dessert. Rich is not averting your eyes in shame when the woman who works in the restroom hands you a paper towel. Rich is bottled water, dry clean only, and valet parking."

Gently cupping his chin in my hand, I looked into his big green eyes. "Do you understand rich a little better now?" He smiled, sticking his tongue in the empty space between his teeth. "Sure, mom."

It was all sweet and good when each of them had one or two dollars to their name, but kids have a lot of teeth. Being fast learners, they quickly figured out how to work the market.

I borrow quite regularly from them, especially from my oldest daughter. She has the most gaps in her smile. If I let her stay up late she reduces her interest rate one percentage point. For a kid who has a hard time keeping her laces tied, she certainly has mastered the art of banking.

The other day she threatened to start keeping her money in an offshore account. Wary of showing me exactly where in her room she keeps her stash, she makes me wait in the hallway to do a deal. The piggy bank on her bureau is nothing more than a decoy containing a wooden coin from vacation bible school that says, "Jesus Loves Me." I wouldn't have been snooping, but late one night Mike and I had ordered a pizza and were two dollars short. Thankfully for us the girls had won a teddy bear at a Halloween parade that was covered in one-dollar bills. I carefully peeled off two from his back and hoped they'd never notice. The guilt gods cursed me with cold pizza, but I deserved it.

Eventually, that teddy bear got so bare it appeared he was molting, and my daughter noticed. These days she makes me confess what I need the cash for before she peels a greenback from the wad in her tight little fist. I remind her that it was I who painted those cute little fingernails, but she doesn't like to make small talk when she's in the middle of a transaction.

According to the chart she keeps under her bed, I'm up to $13 in arrears. I attempt to stammer out an explanation of where it went as she cocks her head and lays a withering glare on me. "Well, we needed milk for breakfast, and Edlen's was running a sale on some boneless chicken." I smile hopefully. "Remember, honey, how mommy always makes your favorite dinners?"

She isn't buying it and stares at me accusingly. "What about that movie you and daddy rented last night? I suppose that was free?"

With luck, I'll get the same Tooth Fairy they had. I'm not looking forward to dentures, but down the road I'd like to be able to finally pay off my kids. The interest is killing me!

3

The Pick-Up Line from Hell

"I'LL HELP YOU ANY WAY I POSSIBLY CAN." MY HUSBAND, always supportive, truly meant it, but I had my doubts he was up to it.

"Listen, Mike. You mean well. I appreciate it. But I don't see how I'm ever going to get some extra writing time with these kids around here. They're noisy and they're needy. Plus, they're bleeders. An innocent game of tic-tac-toe will cause a paper cut that ends up disrupting me for 30 minutes."

He put his arm around my shoulders. "Trust me. I'll keep them out of your hair so you can concentrate."

He's a good man, but as I stared at him with furrowed brows, I was worried. Especially when he said, "Besides, isn't it about time they start doing more on their own?"

I gave a quick laugh. "Like what? Showering? No.

11

Driving themselves to and from school, sports, and ballet? No. Dressing themselves? Maybe. But McKenna puts shirts on backward and Dylan once got stuck in her sweater for an hour before anyone heard her muffled cries, so that's probably a year off. And Sam is like you—he'll wear whatever's closest to his bed. That could mean shorts in January."

He shook his head. "Okay, these are poor examples— what about entertaining themselves? I used to play for hours after school, outside, without any problem at all. It's a matter of trust, believe me."

I sighed. I had a hard time hearing this from the man who accidentally sledded across eight lanes of traffic on the interstate at age six.

"You cracked your head open three times before you reached 10 and jumped in a lake at age 8, sending you to the emergency room covered in chiggers. Believe me, honey, there is no way our kids are 'entertaining' themselves after school. I have a strict regimen of snacks then homework, then a nice supervised playtime until dinner is ready."

He interrupted me. "Exactly. All of these things involve you. You could easily streamline your operation if you just loosened up some rules. I'll give you a quick example. They could get their own snacks and sit down for 15 minutes without you having to be in the room. See? There's an extra 15 minutes you didn't even know you had."

Now I laughed out loud. "Oh, like you did? You got your own snack, sure. I remember that story. You and your friend

Joe used to come in from playing outside and without even washing your disgusting boy hands you'd reach into the refrigerator and grab some raw meat and throw a burger on the grill."

I looked him square in the eyes. "Is that what you want for our children? Some unsupervised time playing on the interstate followed by raw meat and fire?"

He left the room, shrugging and mumbling about how I only remember his stories when I want to use them against him. He knew I was right, of course. After 14 years of marriage, you tend to remember the stories that involve fire and chiggers.

I did feel a little bad, though. After all, how many fathers willingly offer to do more with their kids just to give their wives a break? If I didn't take him up on it, he might not ask again.

If he was going to help, it made sense to break him in on the hard stuff first.

Most of us know that, birthday parties aside, the school pickup is one of the most dangerous arenas a parent can enter. He was a brave man, though. After five years in the military I figured he had the stomach for it.

Armed with flow charts containing maps, a list of children's names, and emergency escape routes, I turned my pointer at him. "I'm gonna stick to the basics, here, seeing as it's your first time." He scoffed, flicking my pointer. "You may be overdoing it just a bit, don't you think? After all, I'm a very competent parent."

I smiled and brushed off the tip of my pointer. "Of course you are. And don't touch the pointer again. I am not going to send a lamb to the slaughter without knowing I did everything in my power to protect it. This information is necessary, believe me."

Thirty minutes into my presentation, I had to tap him on the forehead with the pointer. "Hey! Wake up! You can't drift off here, or you'll miss something vital and we'll never see our children again." I could tell by the resentful stare that he thought I was making this difficult on purpose. Husbands have no idea just how complicated our routines can be.

"Now, let me continue. This is the area of greatest importance. Because you either have to get there an hour ahead and wait in line behind the people who act like they're camping out for Springsteen tickets, or you chance it, show up two minutes before the bell rings, and double-park. The principal shoots you a dirty look and I always wear my best lipstick so the cops won't ticket me, but you might be able to pull it off as a first-timer. You can't park on Broadway, because the doors don't open on the rear passenger side, remember? The kids will get run over if you do that. What you want to do is circle the school, waving one arm wildly out the window so the kids see you, then make a quick right down Grand Avenue where you can quickly double-park and have them get in on the left-hand side. Otherwise, you're screwed and you won't get to them until the anal parents who park six hours in advance leave, and by then the kids will be crying because they'll think you forgot them."

He was staring straight ahead.

I tapped him on the arm. "Did you get all that?"

He threw his head back dramatically. "Yes, yes, yes! Springsteen tickets, doors don't open on the passenger side, stick your arm out the window or the kids will cry. The principal wears lipstick. Got it. Can I go now?"

I said a quick prayer under my breath. "Sure. Just don't forget to pick up the Falana boy. I keep him until 3:45 on Fridays. You can let him sit up front because he weighs more than eighty pounds and they won't arrest you for not having him in a booster seat. Oh, and don't turn on the heat; he's allergic to the dust in the vent and he'll sneeze all over you. Last time, he sneezed so hard he hit his nose on the dashboard and bled all over the extra sandwich I keep in the front seat for emergencies. Sam's gag reflex kicked in and he threw up in his book bag. I had to order an extra math book. Darn thing cost me 12 bucks."

He stared at me, incredulous. I tell you, they think we make this stuff up.

I sighed and rubbed the back of my neck. "Trust me. I wouldn't even bring all this up if I weren't worried about your sanity. I happen to love you, you crazy fool, and I'd hate to see anything happen to you."

After a quick kiss, I said another prayer and waved good-bye. He was doomed. The school grounds were killing fields for virgin parents who had never done a pickup before. His only hope was that someone would take pity on him.

As I heard the familiar thud of our old car bottoming out on the driveway, I wiped away the beginning of a tear. I might never see my gorgeous man again.

After a few minutes I was able to shake the images of singles cruises out of my mind and sat down at the computer to work. I'm not stupid. There was no way I was going to waste this time alone doing anything other than writing. Fifteen minutes or so went by, and I started glancing every second at the tiny clock at the bottom of the monitor.

Various scenarios shot past my eyes. Maybe the train came through town, which is not unusual for this time of day, and he inched up too close so the kids could wave to the conductor. Maybe he stopped to help a turtle cross the street—again not too unusual for my caring husband—and he forgot where he left the car. Maybe he picked up the wrong kids. After all, they sort of look the same when they wear hats and scarves. By the time he returned for the real ones the school might have figured out that we were unfit parents. Maybe, right this very minute, my precious children were being split up into various foster homes around the country!

I had to laugh. I knew I was being just a tad ridiculous. It was probably something benign like the kids playing their cute game, "Pretend Not To See Our Parent Waving And Get Extra Time Playing On The Schoolyard."

Thirty-five minutes later the thud returned to the driveway. I sighed with relief. As they came crashing through the front door I was met with hugs and kisses.

I immediately questioned Mike on the delay. "What happened? Did they get you for not having a note to pick up your own kids? Was it Jump-Rope-For-Hearts Day and they closed the parking lot? For God's sake—what took so long?"

"Daddy forgot Sam!"

My husband, pale as a ghost, gave McKenna a gentle shove toward the kitchen. "Did not! I was getting honked at so I pulled around again. I was coming back for him, but he got all worried for nothing. My God, it's not like they were ready to stick his picture on a milk carton or anything. It went fine. As a matter of fact, it was easy. I think you make too big a deal out of things."

Poking her head out of the kitchen, McKenna whispered to me, "Mommy, I saw another boy get out of the car when daddy came back for Sam. I think he picked up Christian by mistake, but with all the book bags piled on top of me I couldn't tell for sure. He gave me a dollar so I wouldn't notice. Can I go add up all my money now?"

As I watched her leave the room, I had a horrifying thought. What if it wasn't as difficult as I thought it was? What if my husband was better at this stuff than I was?

Then I laughed to myself. Nah. There's no way. It was just as challenging for him as it was for me. Men are just too stubborn to admit it, that's all. I peeked around toward the living room and saw him sprawled on the couch, waiting for Oprah to come on. Just like I do on a stressful day.

He looked pretty cute, even with that nervous tic I recognized so well. Maybe I'd let him touch my pointer after all.

4

Lucky Us

THERE'S A NEW WAVE OF TEACHING THAT TRIES TO INCORPORATE a child's home life with his life at school. Most parents seem to like the concept, although it took me by surprise the first time we experienced it.

My son was the first to get Lucky. The furry stuffed animal had been home on weekend leave with other first-grade families during the new school year, but not ours. Until now.

Sam was almost bursting from the excitement. This from the kid who has lost every stuffed animal he's ever had, and threw one right out the window to see if it would bleed. "I got Lucky! This whole weekend we get to do fun things with him and write about it in the journal, and then I get to read it to the class on Monday!"

I panicked. This was supposed to be my weekend to write. Fighting the waves of nausea I grabbed him by the shoulders. "You're kidding, right?" I yelled into the kitchen where Mike was getting their snack. "Mike, please tell me he's kidding."

He poked his head around the doorway. "Nope. But don't worry. We'll do one or two fun things together as a family and then you can spend the rest of the time writing."

He obviously didn't understand. The cute little pooch and his incriminating journal would provide hard evidence that our family was a sham. For the rest of the school year, more than 20 local families would be critiquing our weekend activities.

After all, our usual weekends are less than electrifying. Every now and then a refrigerator magnet will fall on the floor and we'll get excited about rearranging all the drawings I have stuck on there, but there's not too much else. One time we thought there was a dead bunny in the backyard, but after we got all dressed up for a proper funeral, it turned out to be a stuffed animal. So you can understand why I was afraid that, after 48 hours with us, Lucky would return to the world of the innocents with a hardened, glazed look in his button eyes.

After dinner I called the family to attention. "Listen up! No making pictures for grandma this weekend using dryer lint. For the next two days, by God, we're going to have fun if it kills us."

One by one, the kids threw in suggestions as I shot them down.

"We're going for educational; yet it must be more fun than one dog can possibly stand."

Sam flashed me a worried look. Leaning into my ear, he whispered, "It's not real, mommy, it's just a stuffed animal."

I stood up, dumping Lucky to the ground. "That doesn't matter anymore! Don't you see, people? It's a test. We've got to document this dog having the time of his life. Our entire reputation as a fun family hangs in the balance."

My daughter clapped her hands. "Oh, I know! I know! Remember last week when we watched daddy clip his nose hair? We can do that again!"

I threw an odd look at Mike. "You let them watch you clip your nose hair?" I shook my head. "Listen guys, I'll be getting out some magazines to search for ideas. If you come up with anything better than nose hair clipping, come see me."

I stayed up all night, surrounded by maps and little magazine cutouts of fun family activities. I pored over Lucky's journal to discover what other students had done with him. It was a sickening display of fun family togetherness—photo after photo of kids holding the stuffed dog and posing with cheerful siblings in happy settings.

Not once did I see a kid crying in the background. There were no "rabbit ears" being stuck behind an innocent kid's head for the photographer. No one looked like they were being tortured to pose with their family.

In short, I knew we were in big trouble.

When the kids woke up the next day, I had already been up for two hours making homemade pancakes. I posed Lucky in front of the batter. It didn't look all that fun, but another family had documented themselves making bread from scratch with him, so it didn't seem completely off the wall.

Instead of sandwiches for lunch, we had ice-cream sundaes with Lucky. For dinner we drove him to a theme restaurant and photographed him wearing a crab bib. He smelled a bit like a fisherman after some flounder got mashed into his fur, but I figured that was the next family's problem.

The next day, I woke everyone extra early. This was our last day with Lucky and I had carefully planned each moment. We were going to visit historic Washington's Crossing, where the father of our country had crossed the Delaware on Christmas Eve.

After a day of sightseeing, where the kids were admittedly a little bored, we spied a man on a Harley. I ran up to him. "Could we photograph our stuffed dog on your bike with you?" I pushed Sam in front of me and smiled sweetly. "It's for my son's class project."

He looked at my husband, then back at me. "Okay, I guess." He held out his arms. I was a little disappointed that he wasn't wearing any leather. It was fairly warm, and he was decked out in a peach-colored Izod shirt and pressed khakis. "Darn," I thought to myself, "he looks like a banker, not a biker." But at least he was willing to work with me.

I positioned the camera. Looking up at him, I urged, "Go ahead, look dangerous!" He just held the dog stiffly and smiled uncomfortably. "Me or the dog?"

I laughed, while Mike pretended not to know me. "*You*, silly! Don't be bashful. Go ahead and show any scars or tattoos you have. It'll add to the picture quality."

He turned red. "I'm a stockbroker. All I have is an old vaccination scar. Will that do?" He spoke softly and clutched the dog for protection. I don't know why he looked so worried.

At the end of the weekend, I finished the last page of Lucky's fun-filled journal and stuck it in Sam's backpack. "I really think you'll get a good grade on this, buddy." I smiled at him. Surprised, he shook his head, "Oh, no, mom. You don't get graded on what you do with Lucky. It's just for fun. In fact, the teacher lets us read it to the class, so sometimes we just make up stuff as we go."

I swallowed hard. Mike left the room so I couldn't hear him laugh. He didn't try very hard. I put my hands on Sam's shoulder and spoke very quietly, a little nerve in my eye twitching. "There's no grade? We just spent half our savings and drove through two states for something that the teacher doesn't grade? We visited beautiful historic sights, and I was too busy writing in the journal to even enjoy them—and there's no grade?"

He smiled and patted my hand. "Nope. The teacher said if she graded the journal it might make parents get all goofy and try to outdo one another."

Oh well. At least Lucky would give me an "A" for effort.

5

Love and Periodontal Disease

I Wanted, Very Badly, Two Distinct Things Out Of My Life: time to work on my book, and the knowledge that my kids were happy and safe.

Unfortunately, as working mothers know all too well, these two things go together like white pants on a little boy. First of all, there's the problem of finding a dependable babysitter we can trust. We are instinctively suspicious of anyone who *wants* to be around our kids—after all, while we adore them, a lot of the time even *we* don't want to be around them. Secondly, we know what awful things our kids do when we're with them and can only imagine with horror what goes on when they're out of sight.

The minute I make any plans to hire a babysitter, I can't help but see hazards everywhere I look. Electrical outlets give me evil winks; brick steps mock my naiveté.

And those are only the obvious dangers. No babysitter is going to check that my youngest has wiped after using the bathroom. Sure, she announces that she's done the job, but if the procedure isn't carefully monitored she'll walk like a cowboy for three days.

The requirements for the individual assigned to watch my three kids are complex. He or she must be allergic to the phone, and can never, ever attempt a conversation with another adult unless they are speaking to a 911 operator while trying to dislodge a Lego from a nostril.

The candidate must have a repeat button, or at least be able to say, "Wash your hands first. Wash your hands first. Wash your hands first," without developing a nervous twitch. She must love sarcasm. She must crave peanut butter—not to actually ingest, but to discover in her hair six hours later when applying for a bank loan. She must have considerable experience as a hooker—of seat belts and lunch box snaps. She must not recoil from smells so intensely disturbing that one might think a stray animal has crawled in and died under the front porch.

Although not a must, it is considered a bonus to have a penchant for anything sticky. A Master's in Crumbs is also helpful, but may be earned on the job.

The ideal candidate will have no expectation of gaining any personal satisfaction from the work. The only permitted reading material is a soup can label. The only allowable television is a show whose main characters have been sketched on a notepad and whose theme music is so annoying that it will take years of therapy to erase it from her mind.

One potential benefit of this employment: hairstyle, wardrobe, and accessories are irrelevant.

If a candidate possesses more than one lap, roughly 13 pairs of eyes, and a sufficient number of hands to do 20 things at once, they're hired. No questions asked.

Frankly, discussing the qualifications of a babysitter is a moot point. It's safe to say that no one is knocking down our doors. Statistically speaking, I think we have better odds of getting hit by lightning. After years of looking for the perfect sitter, I may be close to dragging a warm body in off the street and lowering my standards just a tad.

Our first experience in hiring a babysitter left me speechless. I'll call her Tara. She was 16, a Pamela Anderson clone. Pam, however, tends to wear more clothes than Tara was when she first appeared on our doorstep. I had a sudden vision of Tara and my youngsters seated on the sofa watching television when suddenly a heaving breast slips out and suffocates all three kids.

The Runaway Breast sitter was nice, but we later discovered that she let the kids eat yogurt in the bathtub and sleep with their shoes on. Why, you might ask innocently, would that bother me? Because a babysitter who lets her charges eat yogurt in the bathtub must be buying time to talk on the phone to her boyfriend. Or worse.

27

I can imagine the conversation that night. Little Boy: "Tara, can I please have a snack before my bath?" Tara: "Shut up! I'm on the phone. If you're hungry, I'll toss up a yogurt and you can eat it in the tub. You know how to get a bath by yourself, don't you?" Little Boy: "No! My mommy helps me. She says I shouldn't be in here by myself." Tara: "Yeah, well, your mom worries too much. Here's your yogurt, just don't let the water get too hot. By the way, where are your sisters? I haven't seen 'em for hours."

You know what else I've realized? Women will happily divulge personal secrets to one another over a cup of coffee and a white picket fence. They'll share e-mail addresses and bank account pin numbers. At times, they'll confess just how much wine they really add to the beef stroganoff. But they will never, ever, reveal the identity of a good babysitter.

I suspect there exists a secret world, perhaps in another physical dimension, inhabited by mothers with lists of available babysitters. I'll never find that place. I'd have an easier time uncovering the identity of Deep Throat, learning the truth about the grassy knoll, and figuring out what it is that Ben and Jerry put in their ice cream that makes me a slave to it.

One good thing to come out of our experience with Tara is my newfound appreciation for "nervous grandmother syndrome." The qualities that made my mother such an annoyance when I was a teenager are the reasons I like her to baby-sit my kids.

Like most grandmothers, my mother is a natural born worrier. Unlike Tara, who wore belly shirts in February, my mother will bundle up her grandkids whenever the temperature dips below 85 degrees. She will never permit them to have grapes, hot dogs, Tootsie-Rolls, or hard pretzels—all items found on her "chokable" list. She'll go so far as to approach a total stranger and knock something out of his hand if it's on the list and he's standing near one of my kids.

I suspect she has a list somewhere of "deathtraps," a word synonymous with my mother. If she does, it probably looks like this:

GRANDMA'S LIST OF DEATHTRAPS

1. Carnivals, boardwalks, and mall arcades

2. Any major city

3. Strings dangling from a hooded sweatshirt

4. An open window in a car

5. Any window, anywhere in the house, cracked one millimeter during the night for fresh air

6. Large dogs who drool (germs and "unmentionable filth")

7. Small dogs who nip ("even a tiny dog can kill a small child if it bites them in the wrong spot")

8. The ocean, town lake, swimming pools, unattended bathtubs, and large puddles

29

9. Paper clips

10. Another child, whom she doesn't know, who has been stricken with poison ivy and has the audacity to enter the general area where one of her grandchildren is standing

11. Permanent markers

12. Straws ("Did you see what happened to that little boy on the news a few months ago when he stuck a straw up his nose?")

13. School playgrounds with boys who like to roughhouse

14. Escalators

15. Bleachers ("An invitation to the emergency room!")

16. Trampolines, skateboards, and roller blades

I know that when my kids are with their grandmother they will have controlled fun, a decent meal, a respectable bedtime, and nothing more. Which is exactly what I want when I'm not with them.

Babysitters who advertise that they will "entertain" my children just make me nervous. I'd much rather they tell me, "Listen. I have no intention of trying to please them. They will do as I say, remain under my strict control at every second, and will not run, laugh, yell, or do anything at all that may injure them or someone else. I will not run around the house looking for fun movies, I will not allow them to sit too close to a sibling so as to stir up any arguments, and I will not wait on them hand and foot. When you return, you will see them safely in their beds, clean, fed, and fast asleep. They may not like me, but, let's face it, I'm not here to be their friend."

Now that's someone I'd hire in a second.

The only solution I've been able to come up with is the dentist. Once a year, my husband and I schedule our cleanings for the same time. The ambience is lovely: pretty lavender wallpaper, a huge television, and an honor bar attached right to your chair with little paper cups. Even more romantic are the matching, facing recliners that guarantee us at least 30 minutes to gaze in one another's eyes without a child popping up in the middle.

Meanwhile, the kids play happily out in the waiting room with a huge box of toys and talk to the other waiting patients, all of whom pretend to be charmed but wouldn't baby-sit them in a heartbeat. I know, I've already asked.

I suppose I shouldn't complain. After all, insurance covers our date other than the $10 co-pay, and we get to view a 15-minute movie as we hold hands and spit. We've seen it over and over, but we don't mind. Sometimes we get giddy and interrupt each other to repeat our favorite lines from the drama. It's called "Talking About Periodontal Disease with

Chester the Cavity" and it stars—well, actually, I have no idea who it stars. Probably a lot of disappointed actors. On the way home, we drool and reminisce about the wonderful time we had.

Who needs a babysitter when you have that much fun once a year?

6

I Am a Second Grade Loser

EVERYONE PUSHES READING TO KIDS, LIKE IT'S A GOOD THING. It reminds me of when my kids were babies, hoisting themselves up on the sofa and attempting to take their first steps.

"Oh, look, look! Little Sammy is trying to walk! Oh, he'll be an early walker, you're lucky."

Lucky? Do these people have any idea how quickly my life went downhill once the children stopped acting as stand-ins for sofa cushions? They were here, they were there—every two seconds I had to get up and go after them, and life hasn't been the same since.

It's just a short hop, skip, and jump from the ease of bottles or nursing to your real profession: short-order cook. As soon as you get a handle on all of *that*, someone goes pushing them to read. Isn't anyone ever satisfied with the status quo?

True, I'm probably as guilty as the next mom of wanting my children to be literate. In fact, I've always assumed my kids would be voracious readers. After all, kids learn by example and I read all the time. But no one stops to think about the effect on a mother's life once her children gain the same ability to decipher information as she has.

Why doesn't anyone think of *us*?

All of a sudden, the kids knew when I was fibbing. For years, I had gotten away with telling them that they were forbidden from going on certain rides at the boardwalk. "Hey, sweetie, it's not me. It says right on the sign there that no one under the age of 10 can go on this ride. Blame the management."

For years, they knew the truth as I told it to them. Yes, my ice cream tasted better than theirs, but my beloved Ben & Jerry's could cause serious allergies in young children. "See this on the back, in the small print? Let's read it together now, 'not to be eaten by small children.' Sorry, but it's the Breyers for you."

I could tell them that the new "Mary Kate and Ashley" movie wouldn't be out on video for another two months. I could inform them that the sign on the ice cream man's truck said, "Sold Out For Today."

Their world was completely within my control, and I liked it.

Then they learned how to read and I was screwed.

It's not just the little stuff—there were some serious consequences as well. They were dangerously close to understanding that I wasn't the one with all the answers in life. I knew that once they were capable of opening a book and getting information, I would cease to serve as guide and interpreter to the vast world that lay before them. I would be superfluous.

It happened before my eyes. All of a sudden, I had to know stuff. It wasn't enough that I had stretch marks, which, if uncoiled from my body, were long enough to lead Hansel and Gretel through the woods. It wasn't enough that I had a permanent stoop from lifting colicky twins over baby gates. It wasn't enough that they got the best bedrooms in the house, the hot food, and the bulk of my daily energy. Now they wanted my brain!

I sailed through their toddlerhood without giving a thought to life's real questions. "Where do clouds come from, mommy?" Plopping them on my lap, with a smile and a stroke of their hair, they were all ears as I answered gently, "Why, from God, of course."

In the grand scheme of things, sure, I was correct. But they don't want the grand scheme of things. They want precision. Hard facts.

The answers that used to get me through the day are no longer good enough for them. Since I'm afraid they'll tell their teachers I can't help with their questions, I usually end up giving myself quite a headache coming up with what I *hope* are the right answers.

In the blink of an eye, they went from asking what kind of animal has matzo balls to pondering life's bigger questions, like, "Does the garden hose really work through a system of worm gears driven by a turbine?"

Whatever intelligence I once possessed has been replaced by a series of blank stares and bribery to get off the subject I know nothing about and eat ice cream. Now *there's* something I could explain in detail—but do they ask me about ice cream facts? Miserable children.

My anger, of course, is really directed at myself. I'm more than a little annoyed that I went through 13 years of schooling yet have no real idea how clouds are formed. My grades weren't all that bad as a kid, so I'm thinking there was a time when I once knew the answer. Maybe my memory has started to go in my mid-thirties. There's another cheery thought.

Or maybe there are just more things to think about now than when I was a kid. When I was little, the only bugs I saw were spiders, ants, and the occasional hard-shelled insect, which fell under the broad category of "beetle." Nowadays, I'm called upon several times a month to identify some odd species of insect. "What do you think I am?" I exclaim. "A … a … pestologist?"

To which my son, a pro in this field, will wince, whispering, "I think you mean entomologist, mom." See what I mean? I suppose that's what I get for being cocky. When they were little, I had visions of filling their heads with my unlimited knowledge. If I had known just how limited my knowledge was I'd have put off having kids until I'd studied more.

The worst are the abstract questions. Stuff like, "If there's a hole in the ozone, why don't they plug it up?"

Questions like that one make me think they might be on to something brilliant; in this case, I seriously considered letting the Commission on Global Warming know we had a possible solution to one of our planet's biggest problems. It sounded quite reasonable to me.

I never feel quite as stupid as when a seven-year-old asks me what a gamma ray is. "Hmm," I say, quite prepared to launch into a lengthy explanation that will satisfy him for the moment. It will obviously be incorrect, but with my advanced degree in B.S. it'll sound good.

Before I can get the words out though, he's found out for himself. "Oh, never mind, mommy. I looked it up in the book. It's an invisible high-energy electromagnetic wave with wavelengths shorter than a hundred-billionth of a meter, emitted by the nuclei of atoms."

I swallow hard. "Yep, that's just what I was going to say."

It's hard not to blame the schools, though. Where do they get off teaching a five-year-old that byte isn't what they'll get a spanking for, but a binary number containing eight bits? I have to tell you, I looked pretty bad interrupting a conversation between kindergarteners who were arguing over bytes, assuming they were talking about the kind involving teeth. It may be the last time I ever get asked to help out on computer day.

Sometimes I come precariously close to being found out for what I am: a sham. A big, fat fraud. For instance, if a child asks me, "Mommy, what does it mean when the man on television talks about drag?" With a relieved smile, I'll explain. "Oh, a drag is when someone is no fun at all. In a sentence, it would be 'Sarah was a drag at the party because she wouldn't dance.' Understand, sweetheart?"

Four minutes later, after much page turning, she looks at me differently. A quizzical expression on her face, she responds. "Mommy? I think what he was talking about was the force with which air or water resists the motion of an object such as a car, boat, or aircraft."

Then, like the last bullet hitting an already dead corpse, she throws me the zinger:

"But you're probably right, too."

I feel tears sting my eyes and I turn my head away as she rubs my shoulder in sympathy. She knows I've suffered a tremendous defeat.

Sometimes I'll ask my children a question, just hoping they'll give me another chance to prove myself. The other morning I walked downstairs and asked, "Who wants to know where babies come from?"

Ten, fifteen years ago, I would have drawn kids from other neighborhoods had I been willing to sit down and tackle a subject like this. My kids' response, however, was less than enthusiastic. One of them scoffed outright and went back to reading, and another said, "Maybe later, mom. Right now I'm telling McKenna about the role of the communications satellite in our global receiver and transmittal system. But, hey, I'll get back to you."

It doesn't take a rocket scientist to see that the situation is only going to deteriorate. I'm already the last person they'll ask, and, if it comes to that, they double-check me against various reference materials and talk quietly amongst themselves. If I listen hard enough, I'll sometimes hear a sympathetic, "Let's go easy on her. Just smile and let her think she's right, okay?"

I used to think I was too smart for my own good. Apparently I'm no longer in danger.

7

According to the Experts, Buying 20 Copies of This Book Will Make You Live Longer (I Swear!)

IT IS A RARELY DISCUSSED PHENOMENON. WOMEN ARE TARGETS for every "expert" in the world who finds it necessary to improve upon something we are currently doing. I've never really noticed this trend apply to the male segment of our population, although many of the so-called experts are men themselves.

Since I hate to be a Doubting Thomas, I actually read much of the advice I come across, as well as the magazine clippings my mother gives me that explain how to discourage a dog from humping houseguests.

I don't want to hurt Mom's feelings, so I stick all her clippings in the glove box of my car. At any given time, especially if my car is due for a good cleaning, that glove box might contain all the secrets that could put me on easy street. At the very least, I would know how to cook healthier, how to buy groceries for $1.95 a week, and why I've never been able to trust a male pet.

I try not to get annoyed that the advice is always directed at women, but it does irk me that experts from all over the world have decided mothers need so much work.

"Are You Pushing Your Children Too Hard?" "Should You Push Your Children More?" "Stimulate Your Child's Mind by Asking Him These Questions Every Night"; "Homemade Dog Food That Will Add Years to His Life"; "Plan the Perfect Vacation for Your Family."

If only I had read these articles when I was younger! My kids would be smarter, my dog leaner, and my family more satisfied with our recreational activities.

Now, on the surface, they don't tell you they're targeting women. But come on, we know the truth. I think it's the women in the family who tend to plan the family vacation, and as far as feeding the pets—well, our dogs could enter the kitchen carrying a banner that says "Feed Us" and my husband wouldn't notice.

It's no mystery why these types of articles appear in so many of the women's magazines. Men, for the most part, have no interest in reading this stuff. The thing I love most about men is that they don't go through life looking for means of self-improvement. So why do we?

The fact is we shouldn't. And you know what? These experts, wherever they come from, don't know half as much as your ordinary, neighborhood mom.

Take, for example, the latest thing to hit the media. Experts now say it's possible to add years to your life by following three simple steps.

Step One, according to the experts: *Use Positive Words.* Apparently, researchers base this on a study of Roman Catholic nuns who wrote personal essays. Those who used more positive words, like "joy" and "hopeful," lived 10 years longer on average.

What a Mother Knows: *Use Sentences That Make No Real Sense But Scare the Living Daylights Out of Your Kids.* Mothers who string together words like, "If you think you're staying up late on a school night, you had better think twice!" realize that we have no idea what it really means, but we don't care. We have to say stuff like that, and somehow the kids know what we mean when we do. We toss out smart little sayings like, "If you crack your head open you are not going with me to the mall, little lady!" without worrying that the laws of physics (and medicine) would probably not allow this scenario anyway.

If we used words that made sense, or were just meant to be positive, our kids would never do anything. If I ask my daughters nicely to turn out the light and go to sleep, they may or they may not. If, however, I ask them, "Do you want to go to Disney World this year?" I have a better shot at getting them to sleep. Of course, this makes no sense, and I don't need a nun to tell me so. Whether they go to sleep or not has nothing to do with Disney World, but it works and that's all I care about.

To satisfy the Step One requirement, I tried abandoning my theories and using positive words as the nuns did. Instead of stringing together some choice words that would make the dog run for cover, I tried the expert method when I spied three pairs of muddy cleats in the middle of the Oriental rug. With a gentle smile, I said, "I am hopeful you will put your shoes in your closet and it will bring me great joy to see them there at the end of the day."

It sounded good, the dog continued his nap, and none of the neighbors covered their ears. The only problem is, it didn't work. The next day, when the cleats hadn't budged an inch, I grabbed all three kids by the ears and pushed them toward the pile of muddy shoes. As the dog dove under the sofa, I took a deep breath and let it out. "If I have to tell you to put your shoes in the closet one more time, I'm going to scream! Answer me! Don't talk back when I'm yelling at you! What are you, a bunch of wisenheimers?"

The experts would probably frown on my sentence structure and content. First of all, no, I don't have any idea what a wisenheimer looks like or even is. And second of all, it isn't sensible to strain your vocal cords over an issue like shoe storage. Save your serious yelling for stuff that could take out an eye.

Step Two, according to the experts: *Join a Gym and Go Every Day.* This must have been written by a man, because anyone who has lugged an 80-pound kid from the sofa to his bed while simultaneously stepping over a baby gate knows what kind of physical work we mothers do each day. I won't even mention the laundry baskets, basement steps, or holding back a 100-pound dog that wants to body-lick the mailman.

What a Mother Knows: *Invest in a Decent Lock for Your Bathroom Door and Use It Every Day When You Take a Bath.* Much cheaper, and if you combine that with a hefty tub of Ben & Jerry's ice cream, you'll be in heaven.

Step Three, according to the experts: *Surrounded By Children All Day? Educate Yourself By Taking College Courses That Stimulate Your Mind.* Apparently, someone thinks it should be easy to fit classes in during the time we're not at the gym, that perhaps by eliminating the wasteful time we spend sleeping we can squeeze them in. You know—since women have so much spare time these days.

What a Mother Knows: *Spend Time Every Day Trying Not to Accomplish Anything in Particular.* This method has health benefits all its own. Lie down in the grass with your kids and figure out which clouds look like which relatives, or help them collect lightning bugs in a jar on a summer evening. Do things that have No Purpose, and discover how much more fun life is. If you really insist on learning something, color in a coloring book with your child and learn just how much they appreciate it. Learn the secret to building a really cool sand castle, or appreciate how wonderful your kids are by hanging out with them for a few hours when they least expect it.

If you are still itching to be ultra crafty, go ahead and make some homemade dog food. The dog will probably love it—just don't expect the experts to roll over for you.

Some people are never satisfied.

8

I Am a Girl Scout Poseur

IF I WANTED TO AVOID AN EARLY DEATH, THE GIRL SCOUTS OF America was the last organization I should have messed around with. I was way out of my league.

There is a special place in my heart for the legion of well-meaning moms who approach you on the school grounds and ask you to volunteer for things. If your kids go to elementary school anywhere in the continental United States you know what I'm talking about. These moms always smile and talk softly to their kids while you are in the midst of grabbing one of yours by the collar and dragging him home while yelling that he's working on your last nerve. These women overlook your temporary outbursts. Armed with a big smile and a whopping bucket o' guilt, they instantly make you feel like a big slug if you aren't volunteering for something.

I can usually avoid these gals by ducking in among the kids as soon as I see them coming. Every now and then, though, I find myself cornered.

I'm not sure why they want me. It's not like I boast about my skills. On the contrary, I'm quite open about my craft deficiencies, which has gotten me out of a few tight spots. I'm incapable of making crepe paper Easter Eggs for the dance. Sorry, but I cannot make hanging Santa heads out of cotton balls and red food coloring for the Christmas party.

I do, on the other hand, read to the students every month, and I'm room mother. If that's not enough, on class trips I'm always prepared with a large plastic bag for the kid who throws up on the bus. This is a skill in and of itself, and it's enough for me. Besides, if I wanted to spend every waking moment with my kids I'd home-school them.

But I couldn't avoid the Girl Scouts. My girlfriend, turncoat that she is, roped me into helping her lead the local troop. She must have read in the "Get More Suckers to Help You" book about a very effective technique to put people on the spot: ask for help when the victim's kids are standing next to her. Some friend.

And what was wrong with her anyway? Hadn't she heard the rumors? Green makes me look irritable, and the only camping experience I can honestly relate was the time my family stayed at a Holiday Inn and the lights flickered.

But there she was, smiling at me with her arms crossed as my daughters absorbed every word she said, then turned to me with hope in their big eyes. I hate hope in the eyes of children—it puts so much unnecessary pressure on a mother.

She was well prepared; no matter what I said she just stood her ground and smiled. As my daughters stared up at me, I stammered, "No, I was actually a Girl Scout once, and sadly they've barred me from ever participating again. It's a legal battle that still gets talked about in courtrooms across the country." To this, of course, she just laughed, totally unfazed.

I kept trying, totally switching my strategy. "Okay," I said. "I was never a Girl Scout. I just lied to you. See? I lack the moral fiber of a leader. Plus, I can't cut in a straight line and I'm math deficient. Did I mention I've never camped?" I smiled. She smiled back and patted my daughters on their heads.

"Well, great then! We would love to have a novice join our fine organization. You'll grow along with our girls and, before long, you'll be a fine example to them. And it's only an hour and a half." I raised my eyebrows. "That's it? Just an hour and a half, and my obligation is over?" She laughed, showing what I swear were fangs. "Oh, that's so funny. No, it's an hour and a half *each week*, of course. Can't wait to see you on Monday afternoon—don't forget to pick up a vest."

How'd she do that? I swear these women are wasting their talents with small fish like me. With their skills, they should be off negotiating peace in the Middle East.

As soon as we got home the girls ran off to tell the neighbors about their upcoming Girl Scout adventures, while I read the literature that had been shoved into my unwilling hand. The multicultural brochure was full of happy, smiling girls who were obviously intent on making the world a better place. As harmless as it seemed, I still had some unanswered questions, so I called the phone number listed and asked to speak with the person in charge. From my many years watching *The Flintstones* I figured there was a vaunted title associated with this person—something like "Grand Poohbah"—but not knowing it I just asked for the "Head Scout Leader Woman."

The woman who came to the phone was very nice, so I got right to the point. "I'm a novice, and I was hoping you could give me some information that doesn't appear in your booklet for troop leaders."

She made encouraging little murmuring noises so I pressed on. "I've been watching *Survivor* on a regular basis, and it's given me some great ideas I think we could incorporate into the scouting experience. For instance, have you thought about having the kids eat food they find in the wild?"

She thought a minute. "Well, they do go on a blueberry hike during our May campfest." I shook my head. "No, that's not what I mean." Apparently this woman wasn't a big *Survivor* fan.

"I'm thinking we might spin a wheel and have them eat bugs and worms harvested from the forest. One or two of the lucky scouts would get a candy bar. This would certainly add some excitement to the campout, don't you think? Besides, according to the host of *Survivor* bugs and whatnot are rich in protein so I doubt any of the parents would mind. I have some other ideas—now follow my thinking here; if they spit out the bug they get a time-out. But, if they swallow, they get some kind of patch—'insect appreciation' or something along those lines. Wouldn't that be exciting?"

I was immediately put on hold. Frankly, for longer than seemed necessary.

A new voice came on the line. "Hello, I'm Jeannette. Kara felt you were in need of, ah, assistance regarding our organization. Um, we follow a very strict and conservative regimen of traditional goals that highlight the values we promote. Basically, this excludes eating bugs. On camp trips we enjoy meals that have been selected from an extensive list of pre-approved dietary items. Does this answer your question?"

This wasn't what I expected. With a deep sigh I answered, "Well, I suppose it does, but let me ask you this: On page five of the booklet it talks about a welcoming ceremony. Would this by any chance involve burning a tissue and swearing allegiance to the troop?"

Jeannette made an odd noise, and I was put on hold once more.

"Hello, I'm Marcy. Jeannette said you asked about a tissue-burning ceremony?"

"Yes, and I've got some other ideas too. What if we held a tribal council each week and voted someone out who wasn't pulling their weight or selling enough cookies?" There was a pause on the end of the line. Finally Marcy spoke. "Okay, am I on one of those radio shows?"

I assured her she wasn't. "Well then, I don't know what you've heard, but I think you may be thinking of another organization—certainly not the Girl Scouts of America."

Her friendly tone was quickly being replaced by something resembling annoyance. "Are you even a camper?"

I laughed at the question. "Oh, gosh, no! Not at all. I do sleep with my window cracked, though. I feel it's healthier." Another long silence, then Marcy's voice cracked as she wished me luck and hung up.

Later, I sat down with the application as Mike looked over my shoulder. He hadn't finished reading the first page before he started laughing so hard I was afraid he'd burst a blood vessel.

"What's so funny?" I demanded.

"Did you read question number 34?" He looked at me, stifling another laugh.

I studied the entry. "Give your level of expertise managing a canoe. Okay. So what?"

Wiping tears that now flowed freely from his eyes, he sat down next to me and took my hand in his. "Honey, you went canoeing once. You swung at a mosquito with your paddle, knocking a perfect stranger into the creek. You told the instructor that what you were standing next to could not technically be called water, as it was the color of burnt umber. You hummed the theme from *Deliverance* the whole time, had a miserable day, and we went home and ordered Chinese food to cheer you up. Remember?"

I tried to ignore him, and filled out the remainder of the form. He was obviously jealous.

I had to hand it to those scouts—they thought of everything. By the time I had finished, all my little check marks were neatly aligned in the No column with the exception of the allergy question, which I answered affirmatively.

Once the weekly meetings started, I began to realize that these women weren't much different from me. They were peppier, and they had an amazing supply of sweatshirts, but they made me feel welcome.

Just as I started to feel in my element, so to speak, they threw me a curve ball. They brought out the cookies. Girl Scout cookies are great—I just had no idea how I was going to unload 60 boxes on my friends and relatives. I looked at my girls. Neither were missing teeth at the time, and they were pale from winter, so I knew the cute factor wasn't going to save the day. Clearly, it would be up to me.

Unfortunately, no one in my family works in a big office, and, let's face it, the workplace is where the majority of these babies get unloaded. My mother bought a box, and my mother-in-law bought a box. That was it, other than the box we bought when I didn't have time to make dessert one night. That made three. This was not going to get my girls the little patch with the busy monkey on it.

After a week of fruitless selling in the neighborhood, I got up my nerve and called the cookie mom. After some meaningless chatter, I casually asked how many boxes the other kids had sold.

She paused for a second, and I heard papers rustling. "Megan sold 150. Brittany sold 80, and Brooke sold 175. The rest are all in the 100-box range. How about you?"

I swallowed hard. "Oh, let's see, I have to add it up, so give me a second. Hmm. There's two, plus another one…" She interrupted me, excited. "Oh, my gosh! Are you telling me you're up to 300 boxes sold? Why, the patches your girls will get!" I broke out in hives. Feverishly, I stammered, "Well, actually, that would be just three boxes sold. Do you get a patch for that?"

The silence was deafening. Finally, she said coldly, "Just return the extra boxes so the other girls can sell them."

I hung up with a gritty determination. No way were the Jarvis kids going to be known as "one-boxers." It was time for action.

For breakfast the next day, I made Trefoils and eggs. Lunch was Polynesian-style, with tiny Samoa sandwiches and a pineapple garnish. Every time I heard a bird sing, I popped a Thin Mint in my mouth. If the laundry came out wrinkle-free, I celebrated with a few Tagalongs. When the temperature broke 40 degrees, I opened the Aloha Chips. If the dogs didn't track any mud in on the carpet, I threw them a couple of biscuits and treated myself to a Do-si-do.

By the end of the sale the girls got their 70-cent patches. I tried not to focus on the $90 I'd spent. In the midst of the selling chaos, I developed a heck of a sugar allergy and was plagued with a nasty recurring dream. In it, a man in a large cowboy hat stands over me, a sash stretched tight over his belly. He gives me the official three-finger salute as he growls in a thick Mexican accent, "Patches? I don't need no stinking patches!"

9

The Sounds of Silence

As a Girl Scout Leader, I'm Always Amazed At The tremendous trust other mothers have in me. With nothing more than a wave, they drop off their precious cargo and off they go. I guess they figure that since we're all in the same big room for our classes, there's not a whole lot that can happen. And when I hold that pointer I must admit I look downright competent.

If only I were that competent and in charge at home with my own kids.

Sadly, I can't keep my own kids in one big room the whole time. No, they have this constant yearning to go outside, use the bathroom, and generally do tons of other things that are loaded with danger. So far, I've realized one thing: I'll probably hit up the cough syrup when they learn to drive. Face it, if a mom can't relax when her kids are upstairs in the shower, how on earth will she cope when they disappear with a two-ton piece of metal and a teenage attitude?

My problem is that my memory is just too darn good. If I didn't remember the kinds of things I used to do on a Friday night in my girlfriends' cars, I'd be much more relaxed.

It seems to be a struggle just getting them to age 10 alive. No one wants to tell you *that* in those beautiful pink-and-blue baby-advice books that flood the bookstores. Most of these books depict a huge, pregnant woman stroking her belly and smiling at her husband. The people who write these books may mean well, but they are not going to tell you the truth. Believe me, the whole world makes money when people have kids.

No one profits when a woman turns to her husband and whispers nervously, "Wow. You know what, Vern? This motherhood thing looks impossible! Did you ever see the zippers on those baby snowsuits? And what if they climb a tree? Are they like squirrels—do they come down on their own? Let's just go get ourselves a whole mess of cats and relax a little, okay?"

The first year, you think you've killed them the minute they stop crying and just look at you without breathing. What is that, some kind of sick game? I've tried asking them about this, but they claim not to remember doing it.

Ages two and three are the bang 'em up years. Mothers of kids in this age group might as well dress them in blue and purple to match their bruises. Then, about the time they reach four and five, you think you might just be …

Out of the woods.

Ha!

This is, perhaps, the biggest misconception in the entire mother field. Personally, I think this myth was perpetrated by kids to give mothers a false sense of security. Moms are prepared to buy into it: After all, it's only natural to relax a bit once a kid has survived infancy, colic, and the terrible twos.

But then, somewhere after they leave age four in the dust, they enter a stage that seems to last a lifetime.

With a sweet smile and an innocent bat of the eyes, they're off and running. Suddenly, overnight it seems, they have discovered that there's a world out there, and it wants them. It begs them to climb its trees. It tempts them with deep, mysterious creeks and lakes. It calls to them with its speeding cars and trucks, and it will never let up.

Kids aren't stupid, though, and I think they smell our fear. They seem to know exactly what they're doing. I suspect they hold strategy sessions with their little friends in order to identify their mothers' weak spots and plan how best to attack them.

I imagine the conversation going something like this …

"Hey, Sammy, how's your mom?"

Sam looks at his friend thoughtfully. "Well, Bill, lately she's been extremely stress-free. In fact, my sister and I were recently *discussing how she doesn't seem to have any new wrinkles, and it's been longer than I can remember since she's asked Daddy to count the gray hairs on her head—so you tell me."*

Bill shakes his head. "Sorry, man. Looks like you've got your work cut out for you."

Sam nods. "It's okay. We're probably gonna release all the safety latches on my bedroom windows so we can climb out to get that baseball I accidentally threw up on the roof last month. Either that, or we'll ride our bikes all the way around the block the minute she gets into the shower. One way or the other, we'll be sure not to let her get too relaxed."

I know the brain cells in the human body start to die off sometime after age 10, but I can't stop trying to outsmart them—it's my only chance at a sane middle age. One of my plans is to have T-shirts made up for each of them with our phone number on the back. That way, when they ride their bikes up and down the street the neighbors can contact me with any vital information I might miss. Tractor-trailer drivers have employed this system for years: "How is my driving? Call 1-800 blah, blah, blah to report any problems."

It's a brilliant idea, really, and I'll bet it catches on like wildfire. I'd love to hear from a neighbor telling me, "Mrs. Jarvis? Listen, your little boy's T-shirt said to call, so I'm just letting you know he didn't come to a full stop at the corner." Lack of privacy be damned—I appreciate any help I can get.

Better yet, I might put up signs similar to those along New Jersey's Atlantic City Expressway. This is actually a series of three signs that target exhausted drivers returning from the casinos: "Stay Awake" is the first, "Stay Alert" is the second, and "Stay Alive" is the third. I'm convinced a worried mother came up with this program and I love it.

I can envision a plethora of signs that could be erected on my street, including "Did You Really Think You'd Get Away Without Wearing A Helmet?" I also like, "If You Throw That Rock, Be Prepared To Spend The Summer In Your Room!" and "Don't Even Think About Getting That Ball From The Opposite Side Of The Street!" Of course, "Go Ahead, Say You're Sorry!" is always appropriate—just to play with their heads a little. They'd never suspect it was thrown in for fun.

On second thought, I don't know that I'd even limit the signage to the outdoors. I can think of some I'd like to stick to the tile in the bathroom: "It Doesn't Count If You Don't Put Toothpaste On Your Brush, You Know!" and, "Give Soap A Chance!"

Sure, it would've been simpler to stick to cats, but since I committed myself to having kids, I know I've got to protect my investment. I have developed a technique, which, while it's probably not foolproof, seems to be working for me.

It's a simple technique, really, and it's based on the theory that strangers are afraid of kids in pairs and groups. Who wouldn't be? I mean, who would be stupid enough to run off with all three of my kids? Heck, if it were that simple, I'd have no problem getting sitters. So, when the neighborhood beckons, I try to keep all three of them outside together.

Of course, this theory only protects them from diabolical strangers; it's not at all effective on injuries. After all, they're kids. They enjoy cheating death as they zip around on their bikes and skateboards. In a group, it's only a matter of seconds before I hear that ear-piercing shriek.

The first few hundred times I heard these screams of terror, I swallowed my tongue and raced outside with the sweats. I've dropped glasses into the sink to shatter, and arrived outside half-dressed. When you hear a scream like that, it means just one thing: one of your little darlings will soon be en route to the emergency room.

Further adding to your panic, they are always hysterical when you reach them. They may be merely scratching an itch, or grabbing at a bleeding, dangling limb. You can't get the details out of them quickly enough.

Within a few minutes, however, you get to the bottom of the screaming and are finally able to take a breath. Then you hear why they screamed for you in the first place: "I just wanted to know what we were having for dinner tonight, because I'm in the mood for spaghetti!"

Your first instinct, of course, is to smack them silly. As in, "How dare you make me think you were seriously injured! I'll give you something to scream about!"

But you refrain. Once you stop shaking, with quite a nervous tic in your left eye, you ask them quietly never, ever to do that again.

There is something even worse, however. Much, much worse. Something that will make your stomach drop like nothing else ever can.

The sound is quite odd at first. It takes a mother a while to realize she's even hearing it, because she tends to live in a world where she believes she'll never hear this noise ever again.

It is the sound of silence.

Silence means terrible things are happening and you're too stupid to have picked up on it. Silence from the kitchen means they are unscrewing every lid from every spice jar in your cabinet. Why, you may ask? Well, obviously because the contents will make perfect grass for Barbie's Dream House.

Silence in the backyard means they've climbed underneath the neighbor's rear deck to find worms and will remain oblivious to the fact that you're searching for them until you've called out the National Guard.

Silence in the basement means they're painting a birthday card for their best friend using a nearly full gallon can of wall paint, which, unfortunately, seems to have tipped over. Before you worry your little self, don't. They'll just mop it up with the clean laundry from the dryer and hope you never notice.

The reason silence is so darn deadly is because a novice will assume it's a good thing. "Listen, Jim! They've gone to sleep already, and we just put them to bed. We sure do have wonderful children!"

Let me tell you, silence five minutes after putting your kids to bed is never a healthy sign—unless of course you've given them a hefty dose of cough medicine. Silence means one thing, and one thing only: This is the time they have picked to disassemble the child-safety locks from their window. Your oldest child is now lowering your youngest out the second floor window by her legs so she can reach the baseball that's been on the roof since last September. Only the dog will hear the child's shoe hit the ground, and you'll "shush" it so the mutt doesn't wake your sleeping angels. Ah, the irony.

If you are heavily sedated, or just an old-fashioned innocent, and have let all three of your children into the bathroom at the same time to brush their teeth, silence is not what you want to hear. Jostling, potty talk, and veiled threats—these are the sounds you're after. Silence? They must be shaving the dog with your new Lady Schick.

Every now and then when I'm strolling past a pet store, I pause to look at the cats. Sure, if I had a litter of felines instead of kids, I'd probably have nerves of steel. Not to mention porcelain skin and the body of a 20-year old.

On the other hand, I wouldn't have so many laugh lines. And you can never, ever trust a Girl Scout leader who doesn't have any laugh lines.

10

Plantains and Automobiles

When There Is Something Wrong With The Car I Drive, anything at all, I put it in the hands of my husband. He may not have set foot in the vehicle for more than a month, but it's understood that repairs and strange noises are his problem.

I'm kind of like that with the refrigerator. It doesn't matter how many years we've owned it, or what Mike has purchased and placed inside of it—it's my domain. I control it and everything behind its mysterious door. Only I understand the class system that governs each food item as it graduates from fresh to leftover status.

Mike does have a role, however, and that is to act as guinea pig for food I'm no longer sure of. Knowing how my family eats, I have to assume that if a given item were decent to begin with it wouldn't have lasted past day one. So, all suspicious leftovers must be subjected to thorough testing and this is where trust enters into the equation. Fortunately, I have a husband who is quite willing to place the health and welfare of his intestinal tract in the hands of his loving wife.

His faith seems to extend even to those times when I'm putting a meal in front of him that consists of three wrinkled blueberries, a shriveled plantain, two spoonfuls of macaroni and cheese, and a sandwich made up of a slice of pastrami on mismatched pieces of bread.

No one else would eat this—I know I wouldn't.

I wonder if, on the day he proposed to me, it dawned on him that he would never again eat as he had in his single days. Could he have had any way of knowing that the woman he was about to spend the rest of his life with would never be able to clean out the refrigerator without first getting some poor sucker to eat all the mystery leftovers?

I have no desire to see anyone sick; after all, I'm a mother. But considering the time it takes to shop for and prepare food, I believe the only proper disposal method is via the gastrointestinal system.

Even I didn't know I'd be this way. Before we had kids, I could easily throw away food we didn't feel like eating. We were frivolous, spontaneous, self-centered youngsters intent on eating only the freshest foods money could buy. I laughed at expiration dates. Why, the food would never last *that* long! We never even took doggie bags home from restaurants. Yes, we were cocky in our youth.

Once the kids came, though, everything changed. Immediately, I started thinking in bulk. Why make a casserole for five when it takes just as much time and energy to make it for 10? We'll just eat that casserole every day for a week until it's gone!

Of course, I never remember that by Day Two in the life span of a casserole the kids want no part of it. On Day Three, these same children get downright nasty if you even suggest eating the casserole, and they'll turn on you like an angry mob. By Day Four in the life span of a casserole, the ingredients have started to take on a whole new personality.

Days Five and Six are ugly. More transformations take place over these two days than during a routine makeup session with Michael Jackson. At this point, I have to jog my memory to remember what type of casserole it was originally. Even then I'm only able to take small glances at a time. You don't want to stare directly at a casserole that has been sitting in the refrigerator for six days; bad things can happen.

Every time that darn refrigerator door opens, I think of starving children. Of course, it all stems from my hatred of lima beans. As a kid, I'd always push those round green buttons under my mashed potatoes. The rest, I'd waste. Right there next to the pork chop fat I'd leave three or four lima beans, flaunting them. Surely my mother would understand that no child could possibly eat *all* the lima beans—it's not natural.

67

But did she understand? No. She'd just push that plate right back in front of me with a lengthy speech about the poor and starving children of the world. I distinctly remember Ethiopia being mentioned because I made a mental note never to travel there without plenty of lima beans in my pockets.

In my adult opinion, this is just too much pressure to put on a kid. How could I hope to get the beans I didn't eat to all those children? I offered to try a few times, but it simply incurred my father's wrath for being a smart aleck.

Well, *excuse me* for trying to end world hunger!

That's another thing: parents don't like it when you tackle the issues head on—they're like politicians that way, and mine sent me immediately to my room. Again, it was for being "too smart for my own good."

Is that possible?

I guess I was born with the primal urge to reduce all foodstuffs to a form that lends itself to flushing. At the same time, something in my upbringing has me convinced that if food is good enough for the garbage disposal, it's good enough to eat.

However, since I have a tendency to get a weak stomach, it's not me who's going to do the eating. Along with plunging clogged toilets, I think it's one of the reasons they invented the whole husband thing in the first place.

Sometimes, I do feel bad about this—like when I make a nice little lunch for myself and offer Mike all the old lunchmeat. He'll stroll out to the kitchen, intent on getting himself a decent meal, and before he knows it I'm standing between him and the fridge.

"Sit down, honey, and I'll fix you some lunch." As he innocently takes a seat, happy at the thought of his wife doting on him, he soon becomes aware that I'm reaching deep, deep into the back of the refrigerator. The only thing that keeps the food items I'm clutching in my hand from being classified as garbage is a window of about 12 hours. More than that and I wouldn't give this stuff to the dog without being prepared to have his stomach pumped.

For now though, it's food that has to be eaten.

Just not by me.

Now he starts to get suspicious. "Didn't you make that macaroni and cheese last week?"

I laugh, trying to get him off the subject by showing a little leg. "I don't know. Last week, this week, whatever." Turning my back to him, I scrape off the fuzzy top part and scoop the remaining two spoonfuls into a small bowl. "Hmm. What else? Oh yeah, I have some fruit for you."

He holds out his hand. "No, that's all right. I don't feel like any fruit."

"Honey, you need to eat more fruit. It's good for you.

Grabbing the hot bowl of macaroni out of the microwave, I place the three blueberries and the un-blackened side of the plantain on a napkin and stick the whole concoction in his face.

Wrinkling his nose, he looks lost. "That's it? I'm starving!"

What an opportunity! Why, he's practically begging for more leftover food. So I make him a sandwich with the last piece of pastrami and the ends of the bread—which have already been moved from one bag to another because, for some reason, they don't seem to match each other. That's another great thing about husbands. They never notice when things don't match, and if they do, they won't mention it because it isn't manly.

The pastrami slice seems a bit slimy, but it smells okay so I smother it in hot mustard and set it before him.

Holding up my hand, I want no accolades. "No need to thank me, I don't mind. Just seeing you eating a decent lunch for once is all I need." I smile at him as he gingerly takes a few bites of his sandwich.

"You know," he says between mouthfuls, "there's a reason I don't eat off the lunch truck at work. Some of the guys have gotten sick because it's not always fresh."

A bit flustered, I blurt out, "Do you honestly think I'd let you eat something that's not fresh? I'd eat all this myself, but I'm too busy taking care of you."

He picks up a blueberry, frowning as it seeps through his fingers. "So *that's* what you call it."

Some may frown on my methods, but I like to think I'm helping to end world hunger, a little bit at a time.

11

Chattanooga Momma and Her Little Frank Perdue

NOT LONG AGO I SURVEYED THE FRAMED PHOTOGRAPHS scattered about my house and realized I was a terrible mother. My children are ready for braces, yet these pictures all depict toothless babies and drool stains.

As bad as I may have felt for not having framed any recent photos, I felt worse about the hundreds in storage. I have no idea why I spent thousands of dollars on photographs of my kids when they were babies. Did I think I'd forget what they looked like? Did I think they were *that* cute?

Some of the poses are downright ridiculous. Whose idea was it, anyway, to stick a perfectly normal little baby in a flowerpot and snap a photo of it? "Oh, look Millie! Tiffany

71

has scampered into the flowerpot again! Let's capture it on film!"

When we had the twins, I decided that photos of the new babies would best be left to the professionals. I could barely manage changing their diapers correctly; the last thing I needed to worry about was taking the pictures that would represent us to all future generations.

The results of this decision are the most hideous baby pictures in the history of mankind.

Looking back, of course, I can see why. The sedatives had barely worn off and a local photographer was already calling me to schedule a convenient time to take baby pictures. I fell right into his lap. There was no sales pitch necessary; I hadn't been out of the house since my third month of pregnancy, at which time I realized I was throwing a shadow the size of Texas. Plus, I had been talking to the dog even more than usual. The photographer said he could come over in two hours and I immediately agreed to it.

Once I'd hung up the phone, I attempted an objective view of my brand new children. Without benefit of a mother's bias, it was readily apparent that these two kids strongly resembled Frank Perdue squinting into the sun. I adored them, of course, but they were as wrinkly as a couple of sharpeis. Why is it we're born with wrinkles and we die with wrinkles? The longer I stared at them, the more I realized they looked nothing like those chubby diaper commercial babies I swooned over on television during my seventy-two month pregnancy.

I started to think that photographing these wrinkly infants was a big mistake. Then I made an even bigger mistake: I took a good look in the mirror.

My, but I was a sight. Three days post-partum, and I had enjoyed only one good shower. My wardrobe consisted of stretched out gray sweat pants that belonged to my husband. I hated to admit it, but I either went with a drawstring waist or moved on to dresses, which would have necessitated shaving my legs. Since someone always seemed to be crying the minute I stepped into the shower (sometimes me, sometimes one of the babies), there was no time to consider shaving my legs. I tugged my hair down over one ear and discovered it was clumped together in a hardened mat. Then I remembered that one of the twins had regurgitated on my head the night before. Apparently I hadn't gotten it all out.

As I stared at myself, I thought of pictures of graceful and beautiful Lady Diana, the late Princess of Wales. I recalled one shot in particular where she was holding her infant son, William. Her hair was upswept in a regal style and she appeared to be glowing. By contrast, I thought it likely that my children's children would look at these soon-to-be-snapped photographs and wonder if I was some bag lady who had wandered in out of the alley.

It was a far cry from Lady Di's wardrobe, but my choice was between my current favorite garb—sweatpants—and my relatively clean, faded denim overalls. I ignored the beautiful maternity clothes that still hung in my closet, waiting to be packed up and passed on to my newly pregnant friend. Like a general on the field, I stood firm, a tear welling in my eye. "I will not regress back into my maternity clothes. I would rather go naked!"

Once I had my emotions under control, I opened the twins' closet and stared at the sweet little outfits that hung there on shiny satin hangers. My babies were premature, which meant they were built something like plucked chickens, and not one of these smart garments fit them. There were white knit rompers and precious one-piece sleepers with yellow and mint green sheep frolicking about on them. Nothing fit, except—you guessed it—the overalls. Powder blue and white denim overalls that I had rolled up and paired with little white shirts underneath. I dressed the babies, then sat back to admire my handiwork. It was no use. The whole effect was pure West Virginia hoedown.

It was time to turn my attention to the house. Mr. Professional Photographer had informed me over the phone that he could easily set up a makeshift studio in our dining room. I rushed around like a madwoman, trying not to feel too guilty for ignoring the screaming babies who were now supremely uncomfortable in their first big-people clothes. I couldn't believe that the room was still cluttered with boxes from my baby shower two weeks earlier. What the heck had

I been doing these past few days? Had taking care of a couple of needy kids blinded me to my surroundings?

I yanked down the faded streamers that still hung from the dusty chandelier in the middle of the room. Wow—I never noticed the dust before. How could I have not seen all that dust? What kind of mother brings her babies home to a dusty house? One who never turns on the light, that's what kind.

It was then I noticed that no one had bothered to clean the large stain on our new floral sofa from when my water broke. I tossed a receiving blanket over the Florida-shaped mark and hoped the photographer wouldn't ask to sit down.

I glanced at my watch just as the doorbell rang, sending the babies into a hissy fit once more and making the dog howl with delight. After greeting the photographer on the stoop, I yelled hello to my husband who was just coming up the front walk from work.

"Don't worry," I whispered to Mike as the stranger began setting up truckloads of equipment. "He's a photographer."

He cleared his throat and raised an eyebrow as he scanned the room. "Yeah, I can see that, but why are you all in costume? I'm telling you now, you're not getting me into something like that. What's with the train conductor motif, anyway?"

I shot him a glare. "It's not a train conductor costume. It's more West Virginia hoedown, if you ask me. Anyway, be quiet, because these are the only clothes that fit your unattractive wife and your plucked chicken children. I'm too big and they're too little for anything cute, I have no clean underwear, and I haven't had time to shower today. Oh, and I may have accidentally eaten a dog biscuit for breakfast, I was so tired." At this point, I started to cry; completely ruining the lousy makeup job I had done on my way to answer the door.

The end result was a far cry from the serene photographs of mother and babies I had envisioned. In most of the pictures, I looked like a shoplifter who realizes she's just been caught on surveillance tape.

It goes to show you that nothing good can come from a new mother looking into a full-length mirror.

Sometimes, when I'm having an "ugly day" and need to feel better about myself, I pull out those photos. I'm not stupid—I never look directly at them: as if I'm viewing a solar eclipse, I glance quickly around the edges of each picture through squinted eyes. As I shove them back into the envelope, I feel instantly and infinitely more attractive.

And after that fateful photo shoot, two things were banned in our household: mirrors and Perdue chicken.

12

How *Do* They Stick Teflon on Nonstick Pans?

OF COURSE, THE PRESSURE OF HAVING INCREDIBLE PHOTOGRAPHS that capture every millisecond of a child's existence comes from one place and one place only: other mothers. We're not a mean bunch, just a little bit like Sunday morning televangelists who, armed with self-satisfied grins and really bad hairpieces, are desperate to inform the world just how much they believe in what they're doing. Mothers can't be satisfied until we've converted the masses to our way of thinking.

Yes, we're a lot like Jerry Falwell, if a tad more subtle. We do our dirty work with a smile, and it starts the very first time we take our kids to the park.

Have you ever been watching your baby in utter amazement when a perfect stranger makes that sympathetic clucking noise? You look up, startled at the interruption, to see a nicely groomed woman with her arms folded across her chest. "Oh, dear," she says kindly. "I see your daughter is still in the sand-eating phase—they say that can cause learning disabilities."

"She doesn't really swallow the sand," you stammer. "She just enjoys painting her lips with it. She's very creative." Then your eyes narrow a bit. "Who are 'they,' anyway?"

Your question is ignored—all you get is the clucking sound again, followed by the zinger. "My little Ashley never much liked to play in the dirt. She expresses her creativity in her bi-weekly 'Baby Art and Me' classes—you should try them, they're marvelous. At end of the year, they're going to have a little graduation ceremony with caps and gowns they've painted in the style of Kandinski."

"Art classes for a three-month old? A graduation ceremony? I don't think that's for us, thanks."

She walks away with a self-satisfied smile and I feel like I've been bulldozed.

Some mothers don't pit their kids against yours, but do feel comfortable promoting their particular parenting theories. Hang around these moms and you'll soon find yourself wallowing in self-doubt and insecurity.

These mothers collect book after book on parenting, and keep up with all the latest theories. They spank because someone in a book tells them they must, or don't discipline at all because another book tells them they shouldn't. They doubt their own gut instincts, and they won't stop until they make you doubt yours.

Sometimes, when these mothers come across a theory or saying that really motivates them, they pass it along. Many of their best efforts show up on my computer screen several times a month. I appreciate that they care enough to put me on their e-mail lists, and I know most of them are truly well-meaning, but I still have to groan when I get messages like, "Every child has been given the gift of a unique self. Have you appreciated your child today?" As I'm reading, a butterfly flits across the screen and soft music plays in the background. It's hard to appreciate the melody because it's drowned out by the argument going on in the living room—today it's about how they stick Teflon on nonstick pans.

Recently I opened a message from a friend I hadn't seen since high school—I couldn't wait to hear what she had been up to. Imagine my disappointment when I read, in fancy pink script, her thought of the day: "The value of your child's life is measured not by possessions, but by the moments spent drying the tears of a friend." Actually, in her message, she forgot the 'n' in "friend," and I had a hell of a time figuring out what she meant by "drying the tears of a fried." At first, I was mildly touched that she remembered me. Then I started thinking.

What could this message mean? Do I want my child to have friends who cry a lot? And if my daughter happens to grow up to be the CEO of a major corporation, making millions of dollars to make a difference in the world, is that a bad thing? Which would I prefer—a child who grows up like that, or one who grows up to be a street urchin who washes car windows for a buck and has time to dry the tears of her fellow street urchin friends?

Maybe, I reasoned, it was all in my twisted interpretation. I was only one in a list of 15 people she had forwarded it to. It irked me that I might be the only one spending all morning trying to figure it out.

After some time, when I had wasted several hours of good writing time trying to forget the whole thing, I decided to get even. I sent her and the 15 people on her list my own cryptic message:

What is a Child?
Is he an image of you?
Is she the sum of what you never were?
Can you let him make the mistakes you made?
When a child looks in the mirror, whom will she see?
Praise your child through his mistakes and love him even more
for making them.

Hah! That ought to get them thinking. If nothing else, there would be a mom out there like me who had yelled at her son for painting freckles on the dog and would feel tremendous guilt. I could almost see it. "Oh, my," she'd murmur, "I should have never lost my patience with Johnny simply because he defaced Fido. I am a terrible mother for expecting him to respect animals and I shall run right to the store and buy him another pet!"

Sure enough, by the end of the day at least two of the people on the list had written back to ask me if the saying was available engraved on a plaque.

I'm convinced the people who send these types of messages are the same ones who like fruitcake, send out Christmas newsletters each November, and use actual thread instead of tape to sew their daughter's hems. Sure, they mean well, but they are woefully uninformed. Everyone knows a good mother resorts to bribery and cheap tricks to get through the day intact. You won't see that on a plaque at the card shop, but it's true. And who needs a reminder to talk to their kids? I talk with my kids all the time! Why, just yesterday the children and I had a lengthy conversation.

"Did you pinch her arm?" "Did she say I did?" "Did you brush your teeth?" "Are you saying I have bad breath?" "Did the phone ring when I was in the shower?" "Did you hear it ring?"

That kind of communication within a family is something to be treasured.

And it doesn't matter how special, how unique your child is, because he will still fall into one of the following three categories:

The Accuser. This child has a finger that automatically switches to a direct point at the sound of glass breaking. He owes allegiance to no one, and would make an excellent witness in a mob trial. Without any prompting, he will concisely report the who, the what, the where, and the why. None of his information will direct blame upon himself, however, even if he has played a vital part in the drama. Conveniently, the Accuser himself does not appear as a character in any of his own stories.

The Denier. This kid has never done anything wrong in his life, including eat the cake, which is still smeared on his face. Facts, proof, and witnesses are always completely mistaken. His eyes are approximately an inch wider in diameter than those of the Accuser, and his jaw hangs perpetually open in disbelief. The Denier has witnessed aliens entering his room and messing up the bed that he made earlier in the day. In fact, aliens are responsible for much of the chaos surrounding the Denier.

The Disappearing Act. This child has a future, all right. He is bound to be a track star of Olympic proportions. Whenever anything happens, even if it doesn't directly involve the Disappearing Act, he will leave the scene of the crime before you get there. If questioned later as to his whereabouts at the time of the accident, the Disappearing Act will suffer temporary amnesia. This child's favorite phrase is, "I wasn't there, remember? How could I possibly know why the cat is blue?"

If one of your kids doesn't fall into any of these categories, it's a safe bet he's an "Idunno" kid. I have one of them, too.

"Why, my sweet child, did you just dive headfirst into the freezing ocean when it's 40 degrees in the sun and I didn't pack a change of clothing?" "Idunno." "Why are you standing on top of your bureau at midnight?" "Idunno."

Kids under the age of eight throw all kinds of curveballs at you. You've got your lisps, your speech impediments, the dropping of the r's—you name it, these kids know how to use it to their advantage.

I've had my kids in speech classes. And do you know what I've realized after a year of this? They don't *want* you to understand what they're saying! Of course, when the ice cream man pulls around the corner, there's no mistaking what they want. These kids can talk to one another; they can ask for something they are determined to have—all with superb articulation. But ask if they've remembered to make their beds and, sorry my friend, but you're in for it.

The greatest challenge is trying to decipher phone messages left with my kids. In order to find out who called while I was showering I have to cross-examine them, employing several dozen graphs and flow charts, and reading aloud every name in my phone directory until we find one that sounds familiar.

It's not my fault I can't decipher any of these messages. After all, my parents didn't love me enough to enroll me in any of those "Baby Art and Me" classes when I was little, either. If they had, I might not get all the details, but at least I'd be able to draw some conclusions.

13

The Cadillac of Coaches

MOST MOTHERS LOVE PREGNANCY FOR JUST ONE REASON: THEY get to buy stuff. Maybe not as much for kids number two, three, or four—but with kid number one it's Christmas, baby!

It's funny how the items pregnant moms gravitate to have so little practical value. Maybe it's the hormones, but we can get excited over gadgets like diaper wipe warmers. This particular contraption's sole purpose is to prevent a cold wipe from ever touching the bottom of your baby. Of course, when I bought the thing I had no idea that when a baby has a mess in her diaper the last thing she cares about is whether or not the wipe that cleans her butt is on the cool side.

We don't know these things yet. Not with the first.

The illustrious "Diaper Genie" also falls into this category. For those of you who may not have one of these sleek white tanks next to your changing table, I'll explain. The unit resembles a smaller, sleeker version of an industrial trashcan you might find in any mall, but the interior is magically different—it is apparently inhabited by tiny genies who eliminate odors while compressing poopy diapers into neat little balls. This might be preferable to discarding your Pampers in a regular trashcan were if not for the special liners that cost a small fortune to refill. After a month or so, our Diaper Genie was sent to the basement and "Diaper Dad" just made a zillion trips out to the backyard to stick the stinky diapers in the trash like normal folk.

When it came to decorating my upcoming babies' room, I went a little berserk—one more countless victim of those annoying magazines that promote the "dream nursery." I soon learned that decorating a nursery creates a feeling of anticipation reminiscent of wedding planning: no thought is given to the significance of the marriage—the important thing is to wind up in the most beautiful dress that was ever designed.

Perhaps focusing on finding the perfect mobile for the crib eases a mother's fear of impending delivery. In any case, I had a limited understanding of a newborn's wants and needs but a solid grasp of my own wants and needs. I was determined that my beautiful babies would slumber in style, getting a head start in the culture department by virtue of a beautifully appointed room.

The reality was that my colicky, red-faced twins could only see a few inches in front of their faces and would have been just as cozy in a clean dumpster.

Even now, with my babies all grown up, it's hard to wean myself from the sheer beauty of the accessories. I find it hard to resist the newborn department in any store—the fuzzy pink and blue rattles do me in every time, even though my kids never had any use for them.

My three have been out of strollers for years but, for some reason, whenever a new model hits the market I'm drawn to it like Michael Jackson to a new nose. I can't help it. They're like vacuum cleaners: Every year the manufacturers make them prettier and more lightweight and I just have to check them out.

My husband thinks I'm nuts, but men do it, too—just with different items. I'm learning to tolerate his sickness at having to slow down whenever we pass a boat dealership, and he's gradually coming to understand that I must check out the stroller aisle in every department store.

Just like when I first tried on my wedding gown, though, the excitement of shopping for my first baby carriage will stay with me forever. Poring over catalog after catalog I narrowed my search to the top five and, finally, to one. It was the "Heave Ho 300, Model #4873 in Cerulean Blue," and I persuaded my husband to go with me to pick it up. As I explained to him at the time, buying your first baby carriage is one of those significant life experiences that husbands and wives must share.

Featured at the front of the store, and reasonably priced at just $89.95, the Heave Ho 300, Model #4873 in Cerulean Blue appeared to be well-designed. It had four wheels and a folding contraption to keep the sun off baby's head. It seemed like a very good choice.

But I didn't love it.

I did, however, fall instantly in love with the model that was perched high up on a revolving pedestal. This thing was huge! With gleaming silver hubcaps surrounded by bigger-than-automobile white tires, it was a work of art—and roomy as all get-out. I figured my husband and I could sleep in it quite comfortably, if necessary.

It cost $275.

It could hold only one child.

We were having twins.

Although quite incapable of doing the math in my head (whaddya, kidding?) I knew it was way out of our league.

Still, I wanted it. Desperately.

I was convinced that having this carriage (or two of them) would make the pain of childbirth go away. It would clear up my skin, prevent stretch marks, and lighten my mood. Actually, the saleslady confirmed this. Keen to my immediate interest, she sidled up to us and enthused, "I see you know your carriages. This is the Cadillac of coaches—you have impeccable taste!"

See, I knew she knew that I was totally taken with it. I also knew that she knew that my husband wanted no part of it. He has something salespeople refer to as "willpower."

I turned to him and said loudly, "If you agree to buy these strollers, I'll give in on the cutting of the cord. You will win that battle. How good is that, huh?"

"But last week you told me a good husband always cuts the umbilical cord—that it's part of sharing the miracle of birth."

With a quick wink at the saleslady, who was wisely saying nothing at this point, I laughed. "Oh, I probably overstated my case—I was really hungry that day. As a matter of fact, if you want to skip the delivery entirely that's fine. Cutting the cord is no big deal—the kids will never know, and we can always tell them you did it. *But we need these coaches*!"

By the time we left, we had written a check for the two carriages and a couple of fuzzy orange outfits that would make our babies look like giant carrots.

Over the next month, Mike couldn't stop mumbling about the cost. "Why we had to buy strollers more expensive than our car is beyond me. My mother pushed us on an old skateboard and it worked just fine." I ignored him and brought friends and neighbors in to look at the beautiful carriages that adorned our living room, displayed behind velvet ropes like the fine works of art they were.

Soon after the twins were born, we realized that anything that gets a kid from point "A" to point "B" without making her cry is worth its weight in gold. The Cadillac of coaches did not do that. The Cadillac of coaches did not fit in the trunk of the car. The Cadillac of coaches possessed one gleaming chrome wheel that insisted on turning the wrong way, like a freak shopping cart at the supermarket. The Cadillac of coaches couldn't be left outside to rust, so ours were retired to our living room each evening, which made me feel like we were living in the showroom of some ritzy car dealership. Before long, I secretly wished I had settled for the "Yugo" of coaches. Of course, I'd have rather gone through labor again than admit it, so I kept my mouth shut and just hoped my babies were early walkers.

Recognizing stroller folly is a lot like realizing that you and your husband are newlyweds living in a shanty apartment in Flea Town, USA, because you wasted more money on the wedding reception than Elvis spent on a lifetime supply of peanut butter and bacon sandwiches. When you have such a revelation you're convinced you'll never make a mistake of this magnitude again.

Of course, you will.

Now my kids are at the age where their accessories no longer seem magical. I try to be enthusiastic, but going to the store to pick out a new skateboard just doesn't recapture the thrill of those foolish early investments. Girls' bicycles are cute, of course, with their crisp white baskets and multicolored streamers. While picking out a bike isn't the same as buying a carriage, it does help get me through the hard times. I know I'm over my craziness, but my husband will be forever suspicious. Not long ago we went bicycle shopping for our youngest daughter's birthday, and were faced with hundreds of choices. "Ooh, look at this one," I exclaimed. "It has a basket for her dolls, plus a speedometer."

Mike furrowed his brow at the imposing price tag. "A speedometer? It takes her 10 minutes to pedal from the driveway to the front walk. Then she hops off to collect all the dead ants she's run over."

Just then, an excited salesman appeared from out of nowhere. "My, but you have exquisite taste. We call this one the 'Cadillac of bicycles.'"

Poor guy—he'll never know why we ran screaming from the store.

14

Dr. Doom

At The Moment My Children Were Born, I Like To Think there was a scenario playing out in the heavens. There, it was determined exactly what kind of child each would be.

When it came to the boy twin, the admissions clerk, an earnest worker praying for a promotion, paused with his pen and paper. "Oh, he's an angelic one, Sir, blond and blue-eyed. You have noted here that he will be extremely active, but will give his parents great joy." He read a little further before looking up with a smile. "Ah, they've decided on the name Samuel, from Your Book. May I go ahead with the rest of the paperwork now?"

The heavenly voice gave approval, and the clerk looked the baby over once more. Biting his tongue in concentration, he had but one space left before completing the form. He felt a sudden pang of remorse, having penned the word "colic" in broad strokes at the very top of the form.

He preferred going with something like "farsighted" or "flatfooted," but he had already turned in hundreds of them today. Still, "colic" wasn't exactly inspired, and would do nothing to help him stand out for promotion in the dog-eat-dog Department of Imperfections and Parental Trials. Nibbling absentmindedly on the end of his well-chewed pencil, it came to him. Brilliant!

Relieved, he filled in the blank and snapped the clipboard shut. With restrained fanfare, he faced his co-workers who were busily thinking up such mediocre maladies as "loses homework" and "bad teeth." His burst of originality would surely inspire them all. Clearing his throat, he clutched the child's folder.

"World, meet Dr. Doom, a child who will see a twister in every cloud shape; fuzz in every stick of butter. A boy who will quote crash rate statistics mere moments before the family lifts off for vacation. A cheerful, smiling young man in command of more incidental sobering data per pound than Oprah."

Seven years later, the little blond boy still made him proud. After all, there were Picky Eaters everywhere; Drama Queens a dime a dozen. The Lisper frenzy of the nineties forced The Big Man himself to institute a freeze on Miscellaneous Speech Impediments.

But Dr. Doom was pure imagination.

Now head of his department, the clerk often checked in on the boy. Peering through the clouds, he saw Dr. Doom climb into the family car. With furrowed brow, he waited, watching as the vehicle moved down the street. Sure enough, the boy spoke up from the back seat. "Hey, Dad? Guess what the dog left under my bed this morning? Geez, I hope that's just a mole on the back of your neck and not a tick. We're going on the Cape May Ferry today, right? That's probably nothing like that ferry in England that sank last summer. Hey, mom, you meant to leave the coffee pot on, right? Oh, and since you're turning back into the driveway anyway, grab a thermometer, would you? I think my glands are starting to swell."

The clerk blinked back tears of pride. They weren't allowed to hand out perfection, but he sure had come close.

15

Hidden Cost #492 of Raising Children: Bribery

THERE IS ONE THING I WILL NEVER UNDERSTAND ABOUT MEN. Actually, that's not entirely true. I also have never understood how they can fall asleep with one hand stuck in the front of their pants. That can't be comfortable. But mostly I don't understand why they always think it's fun to drive with kids.

My in-laws had surprised us with plans for a wonderful trip to Disney World, and it was just nine months or so away. After considering the various options for getting all five of us from the State of New Jersey to the State of Florida, we were in a State of Confusion.

Mike, however, thought we should just simplify things and drive.

"We'll leave around bedtime on Friday night, and drive all night and through Saturday. You can sleep while I drive. It'll be great! I estimate that we'll get there around dinnertime on Saturday night. It'll be an adventure, and the kids will get to see a little bit of the Eastern seaboard."

He looked so hopeful that I hated to crush his joy, but it had to be done. And who were we, anyway—the Mario Andretti family? He had to realize that there was no way we were getting from New Jersey to Florida over the course of one 24-hour period. It wasn't going to happen.

I started with the facts, and kept emotion entirely absent from the conversation. Laying my hand on his arm, I gently spoke. "Do you remember the last time we paid for a babysitter?" He nodded, and I could tell he wasn't quite certain where I was going with this. "We were driving from our house to the seafood place in Deptford. It's about 30 minutes away, and we got lost three times. You were certain we needed to pass a giant oil refinery on your left, and swore that we hadn't gotten to the right exit yet. The man at the gas station you finally asked for directions from told you which way to go, and you insisted he looked shady and was trying to lead us down a dead end street. We ended up getting there an hour late and having to pay the babysitter overtime. Remember?"

The arm was immediately pulled out from underneath mine. Insulted, he looked me square in the eyes. "No. I remember getting us there, *despite* getting crappy directions from the guy at the gas station. We weren't an hour late; we were more like 10 minutes late, and I was right. The oil refinery was on my left. It was just hidden by that new wall they put up as a sound barrier. I can't believe you'd turn on me like this!"

I let out a deep sigh. "I'm not turning on you. I just know that it takes us longer to get places than you'll ever admit. Honey, I've gone on a five-minute run to the bank that took hours. There are trips to the bathroom to factor in, bleeding, you name it—it happens once they sit next to each other in the back seat. Face it; the kids do not do well on long car trips. They're a little young still, you know."

He scoffed. "That's silly. You underestimate their excitement. Sure, they may get cranky on a trip to the beach for the day, but this is a weeklong vacation we're talking about! How excited do you think they're going to be with that kind of fun ahead of them? Personally, I can't wait to spend time together. We'll play license plate games, and they can help with the map. It'll be fun, you'll see."

I know better. When my kids get in the car, they feel as warm and fuzzy toward one other as North and South Korea. Forget what those sappy parenting manuals say about road trips with kids—writers of such material are clueless. I first began to suspect the truth when, about 10 minutes after I'd bought my first baby shade for the car window, one of the twins removed it from its little suction cup holders and hit me over the head with it.

Maybe it's just my kids—I'm at peace with admitting that they may not be normal. They find no entertainment value in spotting out-of-state license plates. They have no interest in playing the name game. They've never invested seriously in the joys of "I Spy." Sing-a-longs are never as fun as the conversations they will have during any car ride lasting longer than six seconds:

1. I have to pee.

2. I pooped like you wanted me to before we left the house, but I snuck two candy bars from the cabinet and you know they give me the runs. So I have to poop again. *Right now.*

3. (Fill in any other child's name currently riding with them) turned on the water in the upstairs sink to wash his baseballs and left it running.

4. (Fill in child's name accused in above) got sent to the Principal's office in gym today and was supposed to tell you that you needed to be at school by 3:00 P.M. today for a conference about his behavior.

5. I didn't have any show-n-tell for today, so instead I told them about that one Christmas when Aunt

Ruby drank too much and threw up in the fish tank.

Equally amusing are the skills they've carefully honed to an art form. These include:

1. Tapping on the window glass just loud enough to make you think you've run over a nail and pull over on the interstate.

2. Discreetly dropping an M&M into a sibling's shirt and loudly announcing that a beetle has crawled down her back.

3. Gasping because you just passed a sign that said "50% off all Beanie Babies," causing you to pull over to perform mouth-to-mouth resuscitation.

4. Singing you a new song, but forgetting all the words, causing the child to pause and repeat, "No, wait, it goes like this" for 30 minutes straight.

5. Either of the girls telling her brother that one of her friends thinks he's cute.

I don't know how they do it, but I can be in the middle of a truly fantastic day. My mood can be bright, the sun shining, and I could have just discovered an extra $20 in my pocket, and they can make me want to drive off a bridge within seconds. The curb I've just pulled away from is still in my rearview mirror, yet I'm shaking. "Why are you doing this to me? Do you know how long I waited to have children? I've been a good mother to you. I learned how to bake apple pie for you guys and I don't even like apple pie, and this is what I get in return? You are miserable, lousy children who live to torment me!"

My guilt trip works for about 10 seconds, and then someone inevitably breaks the silence to blame the person sitting next to them. Then all hell breaks loose again and I swear I'll never again leave the driveway with all three kids unless I'm highly sedated.

Even worse, the entire universe is against me. Magazine after magazine is loaded with all kinds of sugary advice on traveling with your kids.

My favorite little tidbit was the suggestion that each child be given a small sewing kit and a piece of fabric to make their own quilt square. At the end of the trip, put them together as a lifelong memory of the time spent together. Maybe these people have an unusually large car, or just really well behaved children, but I disarm my kids outside the car before they have a chance to hide weapons that could seriously alter our travel plans.

I line them up curbside, going through a litany of questions as quickly as possible. Through the years, I've streamlined the process down to about 25 seconds.

"Any pencils or pens not tucked away in book bags?" (It's important to look them in the eye during the questioning). "Okay, fine. Any open wounds that may bleed on someone? Good. Any paper clips, bottle caps, small rocks, pebbles, or anything else in the stone family? Wonderful. Does anyone have, in their hands, socks, or book bag, any substance that when combined with travel will be stuck in the hair of the person traveling next to you? Anyone sneak in any insects, small animals, or class pets? No? Terrific! Um, last but not least, has anyone whittled any instrument into a sharp, potentially dangerous object that you will propel into the front seat as I drive in heavy traffic? No? All right, you may now enter the vehicle."

This may sound like dialog from a bad episode of *Cops*, but it's completely necessary for the safety and well being of the occupants of my vehicle, as well as the occupants of other vehicles we may encounter.

Another cute bit of advice is to indulge in family sing-a-longs. When the kids were tiny, this did work out pretty well. We'd pop in a "Barney" tape and, although it had the odd side effect of making Mike and me want to register for a gun, it kept them happy for a little while. But by age five or so, kids have no interest left in such songs. By then, they're like miniature truck drivers with bad attitudes. They want lyrics that include the words "butt," "fart," or "poop." Since most songs don't contain lyrics like that, they tend to alter regular songs to fit their twisted agenda. Therefore,

103

singing only has a life span of about five minutes before it goes completely into the gutter, making me wonder tearfully how the Osmonds and Jacksons ever got started.

So, to help Mike fully comprehend the hazards attached to driving with three young children for 24 hours straight, I offered him a preview.

"Take them to the bank, then drive all the way to your parents' house and drop off the serving dish your mom's been asking about since Thanksgiving. I'll be here, writing away."

He cocked his eyebrow at me. "It's the first of the month, and an hour from closing time on a Friday at the bank. Do you have any idea how crowded the drive-through is going to be?"

I smiled. "Of course I do. That's the whole point. If you can get through the next two hours without pulling off the road and abandoning the car with the kids still in it, well, then I'll admit we can probably make it all the way to Florida with our sanity intact. If not, then we take the train. Deal?"

As we shook hands, I noticed little beads of sweat forming on Mike's forehead. I almost felt sorry for him. He is truly a sweet man and I bear him no ill will, but for the sake of the family this had to be done.

He was gone quite a while, but just as I started to really worry they came bursting through the front door. To my surprise, Mike appeared calm. Plopping a big pizza box on the kitchen counter, he turned to me with a smile. "Did you get some time to write? You sit down. I'll get plates for the pizza."

As my eyes shot from child to child, I was confused. They all appeared content. No dried tears were evident on their faces, and not one of them was rubbing a limb that might have recently been pinched. There was no tattling, no drama, nothing. Just three cute little kids, munching on pizza as their dad laughed with them.

I pulled McKenna to the side. "All right, now tell mommy the truth. Why is everyone being so calm and nice to each other?"

Wiping pizza sauce from her nose, she shrugged. "I don't know. We just love each other, mommy. Part of being a family is spending time together, enjoying each other's company. Some kids don't get to do that. We're really lucky, you know."

I had to grab the end of the kitchen counter to keep from falling over.

Next I tried Dylan. I bent over her little pigtails and whispered into her ear. "All right, listen. I'll pay you one whole dollar to tell me exactly what is going on here."

I stared her straight in the eye, waiting for a guilty response. She just smiled. "It'll cost you way more than that, mommy. I already have tons of dollars from daddy."

I bit my lip for a moment before pressing her. "What do you mean you have tons of dollars from daddy?"

She pulled me closer and whispered loudly into my ear. "Well, he paid us each one dollar for every ten minutes we were good. We were so good! By the end of the trip, I got my pockets full and he said you'll take us to the toy store tomorrow to spend it!"

Straightening up, I glared at Mike, happily stuffing his face. So, a smart guy, eh?

I was about to say something when I suddenly realized how happy the kids were. Mike seemed relatively stress-free. I guess his method was pretty effective, after all.

Later, I snuck into my top desk drawer where I had been putting away money for our vacation in a small white savings envelope. Grabbing a black marker, I crossed out the words, "Shopping Fund" and wrote, "Miscellaneous Bribes."

The parenting magazines wouldn't approve, but what do they know anyway?

16

It's a Sickness

"I Don't Want To Alarm You, But I Think I'm Sick. In Fact, I'm half tempted to walk toward the Light."

I smiled wanly at Mike, willing him to do something to take away the pain. "My throat hurts, my glands feel like two goiters, and my bladder seems to have shrunk to the size of a pea. Either my ankles have doubled in size, or my vision is blurred. I can't remember if I'm supposed to worry about radiating pain in my left arm or my right, but since they both ache, it doesn't much matter. As I lay here moaning in pain, I'm worried that if I die you'll have to do the girls' hair and you'll pull their pigtails too tight resulting in nerve damage."

Giving me a cursory glance, he did what he always does. Shrugged off my agony like a cheap suit. "I had the same thing last weekend, only I didn't mention anything to you because I had so much yard work to do. I was able to get through it. You know what helped me? Positive thinking. I just made up my mind that I wasn't going to let it get the best of me."

Through blurred eyes and half-shut lids, I looked up at him. "Gee, thanks for the sympathy. You're about as caring as our kids. A few minutes ago I had to punish them for setting up the checkerboard on my back. McKenna propped both legs up on my chest and told me if I was well enough to blink then I could certainly tie her shoes. What is wrong with you people? Don't I take care of *you* when *you're* sick?"

He chuckled. "Are you comparing us? Because you know I don't get sick very often. When I do, like I said, I just make up my mind that I'm not gonna let it get me down. That's what you have to do, you know—concentrate on something else to take your mind off how rotten you feel."

Although my eyes were still blurred with sickness, I managed to focus on him for a second. "Are you kidding? The last time you got the flu you pulled out our insurance policy and told me to save your razor clippings so the kids would have something to remember you by."

He scoffed. "That was at least two years ago. And you have to admit I looked pretty bad. I mean, I was *really* sick."

I laughed softly, despite the shooting pains in my head when I moved even slightly. "Yes, I remember. You slept on the sofa with the portable phone and called me every five minutes. I finally took the battery out when you called me while I was upstairs putting the laundry away. If I remember correctly, you asked me if I'd ever remarry and, if so, would it be anyone you knew."

He sniffed. "I was just taking my illness seriously for once. After all, you know how high my pain threshold is. If I was in that much agony, can you imagine what that would have done to someone like you? I'm just glad it hit me instead."

That's the problem with stoic men like my husband. When these guys get sick, which admittedly is rare, they believe they've somehow contracted a mysterious, never before identified virus. Since no one else has ever been known to suffer from this particular illness they repeat over and over how glad they are it struck them and not you. All *you* need when you're sick, however, is a healthy dose of positive thinking. Typically, they're under the impression that it's "just your period." Either it's coming on, going away, has lasted too long, or hasn't arrived; no matter what time of the month it actually is, it will be the cause of whatever is wrong with you.

My period has been blamed for everything from bunions to tonsillitis.

He rubbed my shoulders in a gesture of encouragement. "Now, up you go. All you need is to get your mind off it. You're a trooper, you just need to focus on something else."

It wasn't difficult to find something to focus on. For some reason, whenever I get sick I have to prove to my doctor's office that it's not all in my mind just to get an appointment. In the past, they've required a legal brief, exhibits, and character witnesses, and I wasn't looking forward to going through that again right now. But I really needed to be seen—there was just no way my array of complaints could be diagnosed over the phone.

I tried to mentally prepare before I called. An hour later, with several throw-up breaks in between the redialing process, I finally heard the phone ring. I broke into a cold sweat like an Oscar winner who's waited 20 years to hear her named called. I was overcome with joy. For a brief moment, I was rendered speechless by the victory, but I thankfully recovered in time to stammer out my name and request.

Asked to articulate my symptoms, I summoned the extra-polite voice I usually reserve for clergy and the elderly. However, my brain seemed to have frozen, leaving me with the communication skills of a five-year-old.

"Um, I really feel awful and I need to see the doctor, please. *Please.*"

The voice on the other end of the line sighed and shuffled some papers around. "Are you a patient here?"

Why do receptionists always sound annoyed? This one had the attitude of a world-famous heart surgeon who was interrupting some vital surgery to answer the phone.

110

As I started to stammer out the facts, I threw in a few lies. "Oh, yes. In fact, I've been a patient there for 14 years—that's longer than some marriages. Remember when you let me come in on a weekend and I brought you a dozen roses and some cookies?" (A big lie.) "No one believed I had really gotten a Saturday appointment, so I saved my cancelled check and showed all my friends. And unlike some people I could name, I have never, ever stolen a copy of *People* from the waiting room." (Another big lie.)

"Hold on."

Hearing that familiar on-hold music once again, I wondered if Barry Manilow was getting his share of the royalties. Still, I pinched myself to see if I was dreaming. I was one step closer to getting an appointment. Despite my fever and sore muscles, I thought briefly about jumping for joy. Then the nurse came on the line.

"Do you have a high fever?"

I thought hard. Should I fib again, and risk her ire? In a frenzied moment I hoped I wouldn't regret, I decided to tell the truth. "I can't really tell. The kids used my thermometer as a nose for their snowman last winter because we were out of carrots. But I think I have a temperature, because the puppy is sleeping on my chest and he usually naps near the radiator."

She cleared her throat. "Hmm. That's bizarre. Any other symptoms?"

I started to get excited. Like Susan Lucci after 15 years of failure, I could finally see the light at the end of the tunnel. "Yes, yes! Last night, I got very worked up because there was a sudden rainstorm and I couldn't sleep because I kept thinking about the moles drowning in our backyard. Plus, I used to play right along with all the Jeopardy contestants but now I seem to be, um, less smart. See? I couldn't even think of a word for it—that must mean something, huh?"

I ended up on hold. Again.

After hearing "Copacabana" and "Mandy" each play twice, I got the shakes. I was overdosing on a lounge singer and felt compelled to sing along, even with my raw throat. Suddenly, a new woman came on the line and introduced herself as Nurse Madison. She was a perky little gal who sounded about 16.

Great. I'm on my deathbed, and Barbie's friends are giving me medical advice.

"Listen," I explained politely, "I really do feel terrible. I have rotten chills, and either I've developed an instant case of varicose veins or I'm seeing blue lines when I look down. I can't tell. Can't you make an appointment for me? Please?"

Barbie's gal pal Madison wasn't impressed, despite her obvious youth. Maybe if I had thrown in tickets to the Backstreet Boys, but who would have known?

"You have an upper respiratory infection. It's going around, and right now our office is full of people who have

112

it. Don't worry, I'll call in a prescription for you." She laughed, a pretty, Disneyesque tinkle of a laugh.

I wondered how on earth all those people in the doctor's office were able to get an appointment. What had they done right that I hadn't? I probably should have just stumbled in and pretended to have been in an accident.

But I didn't share this thought with little Miss Madison— after all, I didn't want to tick her off just before flu season. As I groaned politely and thanked her, she was kind enough to leave me with a parting piece of advice.

"Just make up your mind that it's not going to get the best of you. You'll be fine after a little rest, you'll see. Think positively!"

I hung up the phone in disbelief, imagining her roller-blading back to her patients while I suffered alone.

Dragging my limp body up the stairs, I rummaged through the medicine cabinet looking for anything that would alleviate my myriad of symptoms. Unless I was suffering from colic, diaper rash, or canine irritability, I was outta luck. If I had a hairball I couldn't work up, I'd be cured soon enough. If I had athlete's foot or jock itch, I'd feel better by lunchtime. Unfortunately for the woman who had shopped for all these remedies, there was no relief in sight.

I finally located some dusty boxes of cold medication, but choosing between them was not going to be easy. One said it would inhibit my cough; the other claimed it would encourage it. The third one just ignored it altogether, but promised to ease my postnasal drip. I gave up after an hour of reading the small print and slumped to the floor in a state of exhaustion. I just didn't feel good enough to do this kind of in-depth research.

When Mike found me there, he tried to help. I tried to be receptive but I had grown quite bitter by now. He seemed to realize this when I kicked him, weakly.

"I don't know why you don't want me to go get the medicine the doctor called in for you."

I kicked him again. "Because it always takes the pharmacy a few hours to fill the prescription—if it's even been called in. I'm guessing Nurse Madison is so busy planning for tonight's Justin Timberlake concert that she forgot all about it. So I need something now, okay?"

He fumbled for the directions inside the boxes. "Fine by me. Just don't bite my head off for trying to help you. Okay, let's see which one of these will make you go to sleep so you can hopefully wake up in a better mood. Just kidding! Hmm, I should have grabbed my glasses. Oh, okay, here they are. Do you prefer sudden excitability or gradual drowsiness that may prevent you from operating heavy machinery?"

I pushed the hair out of my eyes and glared up at him. "I don't know—surprise me."

He read on. "All right. Do you currently take any MAO inhibitors? Probably not. Okay, well, this one sounds okay. There is a possibility, however, that you may experience loose bowels, diminished vision, an unhealthy desire to urinate, and a craving for salt. It may cause temporary stiffness in your joints, an inability to articulate your thoughts, and hair loss. Oh, and you'll probably experience some bloating and difficulty swallowing due to an excess of saliva."

The side effects sounded worse than what I had in the first place. I started to shake my head in protest. "I don't know. Maybe I shouldn't take anything. I mean, hair loss?" I ran my hand over my head protectively.

He shushed me. "You worry too much. Besides, what're the chances of getting these side effects, anyway?"

He started to pop the cap, then stopped suddenly. With narrowed eyes, he read one last side effect. "Wow. Wait a minute—this is why you should always read the fine print. See this?"

I blinked hard as he pushed the bottle into my face.

"No. I can't focus right now, seeing as I'm in the midst of a migraine. Why don't you read it to me?"

He exhaled dramatically, shaking his head slowly. "And to think I almost gave you two of these!"

Grabbing the bottle from him, I read the last sentence on the back with great effort. "Side effects may include a reduced sex drive."

I opened it and quickly popped two of the pills in my mouth. I smiled widely after swallowing. "Hey, I wouldn't look so worried if I were you. All you need is a little … come on, you know what I'm gonna say, now, don't you? That's right, it's called *positive thinking*."

Whoever said laughter is the best medicine sure knew what they were talking about.

17

The Circus, er, Circle of Life

THIS MAY SOUND AWFUL, BUT HEAR ME OUT: THERE REALLY IS not that much difference between children and pets.

Think about it. Both need shots, both must be trained not to pee on the floor, both go nuts when company comes, and both cost more than you ever expected. If you weigh their various strengths and weaknesses you may still come up confused as to which is the smarter investment. Me? I have both, for the sake of variety.

Since human pets, also referred to as "children," are completely unpredictable, I lean toward animal pets of the normal variety. I know some pet owners swear by snakes and lizards, and others love weasels and parrots and pot-bellied pigs, but dogs and cats are more my style. I might be persuaded to buy a well-behaved fish, but even that would be a pretty hard sell. You see, my one foray into creative pet keeping did not work out, and I will not make that mistake twice.

The name was Hermie NMI (No Middle Initial) Jarvis, and he came into our family quite by chance. A couple of years ago, while browsing through the toy store before Christmas, I stumbled upon a section featuring all kinds of interesting items for children who appreciate nature. Seeing as my own little urchins just adore digging up worms, will chase a butterfly for blocks, and are fascinated by birds, it seemed I'd hit the mother lode.

First I looked at the butterfly kits, but the image of a striped caterpillar on the back of the box led me to suspect that I'd be paying 40 bucks for a glorified worm in a fur coat. As you might have deduced by now, I've never been one of those moms who gladly holds out her hand to experience the joy of a bug. No, I'm more the kind of mom who runs with arms waving high in the air as my kids chase me, convinced I must want to hold the small, fuzzy creature they've found on a leaf.

Next on the shelf was a variety of ant farms, ranging in size from your basic "gentleman's farm" to lavish spreads that made me quite envious. Anyway, I decided it would be nuts to pay good money to bring these little critters into a house where I once paid good money to have the same critters, well, as the Sopranos would say, "whacked." Plus, there's that whole labor thing with farms, and the migrant worker issues to deal with. Frankly, this stuff worries me, so I kept walking.

Then I came upon something that looked like a tropical island. It was lovely, actually. Although it was made of plastic, it had a sandy beach area, bordered by deep pools that the owner of the island apparently fills with water. There were fake palm trees, a little cabana, and what appeared to be a tiny thatched tiki bar. Now *this* was the nature experience I was looking for!

Maybe it was the 20-degree temperature outside, or the wonderful memories of our honeymoon spent largely at a tiki bar on a South Florida beach, but I was hooked.

A bonus was the limited effort required to get up and running. Apparently, once we'd filled the pools with water the little inhabitant could swim and enjoy the plastic beach all day. Even if I had to rub the wee fellow down with miniature bottles of sunscreen, I felt certain I had just picked the ideal gift for my kids.

I lugged it home and showed it to Mike, who said, "You do realize this is a frog habitat, right?" I laughed. "Of course I did!" I hadn't quite put it all together in my head, but I would have figured it out. Still, I wasn't thrown. Frogs are cute, they don't fly around, and if they escape, well, they're not going to reproduce unless they can find another frog in the house to date. My kids had grown up on Kermit, I reasoned, and he's harmless enough. He sings, holds intelligent conversations, and has a sense of humor to boot.

119

I turned the box upside down and shook it. No frog. I held it up to my eye and peered inside the dark space. Nothing.

"All we have is the island? Where does the frog come from?"

Mike laughed. "What, did you think he'd fly in from Bermuda? We have to send away for him. That's what these forms are for. Apparently, and I only know this because *I read the directions,* you fill these out for as many frogs as you want, and in about three weeks, you get your tadpoles in the mail."

Seeing my confused expression, he shrugged. "I'm sure it's easy. They give you a little plastic cup to keep the tadpole in until he becomes a frog, which, according to the pamphlet, takes about a month or so. Each tadpole costs a dollar, and you pay about five bucks for shipping and handling. If we mail it out today we should get the shipment by Christmas."

I shook my head in despair. I wasn't upset about the cost. I wasn't even upset about the thought of not having the tadpoles home for the holidays. I was upset because I would be responsible for raising a tadpole into a frog. More mothering—and I had paid money to do it!

I rolled my eyes. "So about the only benefit to this whole deal is that I get away with no stretch marks? I wanted the frog to be able to use his island getaway right away. I wanted the kids to have a present they could use. Now I find out I've purchased a pet whose primary residence, for the most part, will be the inside of a Dixie cup. Gee, what fun!"

We discovered something else, too. After Christmas morning had come and gone with no tadpole, and we had our children unwrap a giant gift that was merely a home for a pet that hadn't arrived yet, we read the fine print. Apparently, when you live in the Northeast, they will only agree to ship Kermit when the temperature is mild, as in spring. Sure, you say, we could have gone to the local pet store, plunked down a buck and bought a tadpole. Not that easy.

The tadpole we sent away for wasn't your regular, dime-store variety tadpole. No sir. We were awaiting the arrival of a Leopard Frog tadpole, a genus not sold anywhere I was willing to drive to. So, you might think, well, okay, buy a regular old froglet and introduce him or her to his or her Leopard Frog brother or sister when it arrives in the mail. Nope. No can do.

Why? Well, I'll answer that. According to the several hundred experts I consulted in my quest to fill the occupancy requirements of our vacant Frog Island, you cannot mix Leopard Frogs with any other kind of frog. Ever. They'll eat each other, or end world peace, or something equally horrible. Frankly, I don't remember all the gory details, but suffice to say it can't be done.

When February passed and we entered the balmy month of March, I grew hopeful that Kermit would soon bless our home with his presence. Indeed, I arrived home one afternoon and

121

found, on my porch, a large square box labeled, "Open Immediately—Live Leopard Frogs Inside."

Unfortunately, that morning had brought a freak blizzard to our front door as well.

Hastily ripping open the box, I found two tiny plastic tubes with a small amount of grayish water inside. Not knowing Mike had ordered two tadpoles, I was immediately relieved he had, because one was dead. As a doornail. Apparently, spending the day in a tube the size of a lipstick on a 27-degree porch is not the healthiest thing for a tadpole.

We buried Mikey, Hermie's unfortunate brother, that afternoon when the kids got home from school. The girls, heads bowed respectfully, borrowed my Bible and said a few words as their brother solemnly tossed the stiff little corpse into a deep hole. Or at least, as deep a hole as a six-year-old can dig through frozen ground covered in four inches of snow. The dog would dig him up at the first thaw, but they'd never know.

After that, we patiently waited the requisite month for Hermie to morph into a frog. Then we waited another month. By the third month, I was beginning to think that Child Protective Services (Amphibian Division) would soon be knocking on my door for keeping this little guy on my kitchen counter in a Dixie cup for so long.

By month four, I was on the phone with the people who had sent Hermie to us in the first place. "Oh," the man on the line said grimly, upon hearing the tragic circumstances of Hermie's infancy. "Yeah, he's probably damaged in some irreversible way from the cold shipping process. That's probably why the other one never made it."

I took a deep breath. This guy was not exactly the zoologist I had been expecting to speak with. In fact, his grasp of the facts at hand suggested to me that he didn't know any more about the growth rate of frogs than I did. Still, I gave it a shot and proceeded. "Um, yes, that's what we think too. My question is what we can do about it. Would keeping him in a tank help? Is there anything we can feed him that might encourage his development? There must be something we can do for him."

He chuckled. "Well, of course there is, darling! Did you think I wasn't gonna help you out? That's why I'm on this hotline, now, so don't you worry!"

I was giddy with relief. "Oh, thank you! I knew you'd be able to help. Now, what exactly should we do?"

"Flush him."

I cleared my throat, and whispered into the receiver. "Excuse me, but could you repeat that, please? It sounded like you said I should flush him."

"That's right, ma'am. Just go on and flush the little bugger and we'll go ahead and send you out a new one."

Running into the bathroom with the phone, I slammed the door so no one would hear me. "Are you kidding me? Because, sir, we have gotten very attached to Hermie, and I cannot believe that you would tell me to just go ahead and flush this poor creature, as if, as if…as if he could so easily be replaced in our hearts!"

I felt a tear well up, and I brushed it away angrily. Until that moment, I had no idea how attached I'd gotten to my little fishy friend in the Dixie cup. We had spent so much time together in the past four months. I was always in the kitchen; he was always in the kitchen. Why, it was just natural that we had bonded.

I hung up on the homicidal customer service rep and wandered back into the kitchen. Staring down at Hermie, I knew I couldn't give up on him. The kids would be devastated.

Oh, who was I kidding? They barely remembered he existed. In fact, one evening I had to practically rip the Dixie cup from Sam's hand as he came close to thinking it was his milk cup.

From that moment on, Hermie lived in the lap of luxury. I accepted his disabilities, and bought him the finest six-gallon tank that $20 could buy. I fed him dried mosquito larvae. I splurged on his one-year birthday and picked up a fake log for his tank, placing it gently in front of the leafy fern I had added earlier to brighten up the place.

Every so often, one of the kids would check him for legs, but they never developed. His tail never shortened, and he never lost his appetite. In short, there was no sign that he was progressing normally and would someday be a Leopard Frog.

I wouldn't be honest if I didn't admit I felt some bitterness. I was sad, maybe even a little angry. After all, why our Hermie? Why should he not experience the same joys as other frogs? Should he not jump in his lifetime? Should he not go through the mad rush of anticipation to catch that first fly on a long froggy tongue? Why him?

And what about *me*? Had I done something to cause his problem? Maybe it was all my fault. Maybe I wasn't doing a good job mothering a tadpole, and that's why he was refusing to morph into a frog. Maybe it was the stress of his environment. I knew I was blaming myself needlessly, but why had I insisted on placing his tank in the kitchen where the kids sit to eat all their meals? There are more arguments there per square foot than in a city block during a heat wave. Had I subconsciously thwarted his efforts to grow legs by surrounding him with bickering children?

By the time another Christmas had passed, Hermie seemed to have accepted a life spent swimming instead of jumping. Then one day an odd thing happened. Two black buds appeared on his underbelly. I didn't want to make him feel like all I cared about was his becoming a frog, so I kept my excitement to myself. I didn't even share my suspicions with the kids.

Three months later, it happened—the black buds became legs overnight.

It was truly a glorious day in the Jarvis household.

125

To commemorate the occasion, I penned a little poem on behalf of Hermie.

Yea, though I have cooked amongst the hum of a filter,
I will fear no more,
For the end of the tail is here.
The sight of his little legs comfort me,
His days of swimming as a tadpole are through,
My fish tank runneth over.

The kids were thrilled. We ran upstairs and dug out his Frog Island, which had finally been stored away in Sam's closet. They helped me dust it and together we read the directions for the new food we'd have to get now that Hermie's mosquito larvae was no longer appropriate fare.

"Wow, mom. I can't believe you aren't afraid."

Sam was staring at me with pride, holding one end of the frog instructions as the other dangled to the floor. I smiled at him. "What do you mean, sweetheart? Why would I be afraid?"

His eyes grew large as he just stared at the instructions. I strode over to where he was standing and grabbed them from him. "I know it's been more than a year since I've read these, but there's nothing here for me to be afraid of."

He let out a nervous laugh and backed up a step. "Did you read the fine print, mom?"

"Oh, now you sound just like your father! Of course I read the fine print, Sam."

126

My eyes scanned furiously over the page. What on earth was he talking about?

Then I saw it. Under the section titled, "Now That You Have A Frog" was a paragraph called, "Food Requirements For Your Frog." Of course I had never read that part. Up until now, I had a tadpole, not a frog.

"That is so cool mom, really. Knowing how scared you are of crickets and all. Gosh. I remember that one time you thought you saw one in the basement and you called daddy at work and told him we had a family emergency and he got so mad because you made him come all the way home! Oh, and remember the time a cricket jumped on your sneaker in the backyard and you ran so fast that you pulled your porkstring and started crying? I mean the fact that you have to give him five to six live crickets a day is awesome! Wow. Wait till I tell dad!"

I just stood there as he ran off. To myself, I murmured, "Hamstring, Sam, not porkstring."

After I read the paragraph again, I stared long and hard at my budding little frog. Hermie and I had grown close, and we were about as tight as a thirtysomething mother and a froglet could be.

I shook my head as I watched him start hopping for the first time up on his fake log. It was as if his determination and my love had made a miracle.

Would anyone notice if I flushed him?

18

Can You Still Give a Kid a Time-Out if He's Taller Than You and Carries a Gun?

THE SCENE IS SOMEWHAT FAMILIAR; YET EERILY DIFFERENT AT the same time. Visible in the harsh glare of the one unbroken streetlight, a tall blond man strolls importantly down the darkened alley. As his shoes make noise on the wet black pavement, he looks annoyed at the sound and glances behind him. No one.

Suddenly, he stops in his tracks then moves to the brick wall of an abandoned building, pressing his body flat against it and silently motioning to his partner. Weapons are drawn, and the two men are on the suspect before the eye can even register movement.

"On the ground! Don't even think about it, pal!"

As the shorter, stocky man hauls the perpetrator to his feet, the blond man shoves a wrinkled photograph under his nose. "Go ahead, tell me you don't know anything about her! We know you did it, Flynn, and this time you're not walking away!"

These are the images I see when I shut my eyes and listen to my seven-year-old boy tell me about his dreams of being a criminal detective someday.

The only problem is, I know this kid. And knowing him as I do, I have a hard time seeing him as one half of Starsky and Hutch.

First of all, Sam hates belts. The news that he will have to put a belt on in the morning will produce more temper tantrums last thing at night than any other issue known to man. It has nothing to do with what the belt looks like. It has everything to do with the fact that this boy, who has taken laziness to new heights, will have to unbuckle and tuck his shirt back in every time he urinates. Knowing that the time involved with such a task may temporarily delay him from an activity for a millisecond completely spoils his mood.

So I naturally assumed he'd be interested in an occupation that requires loose, baggy clothing that never needs tucking in. A gardener, perhaps, or a beachcomber, or maybe even a Navy pilot in a one-piece jumpsuit; this is how I have pictured my son making his future living.

It is equally difficult for me to imagine Sam handling a weapon. We've never bought him anything other than water pistols, but being a typical boy he uses various sticks as well as his index finger whenever he's in need of a gun.

Unfortunately, he misplaces everything he touches. He can be given four quarters for the ice cream man and if it takes the truck longer than two minutes to get around the corner to our house, one will already be missing. I would swear in a court of law that I never saw him budge from his place at the curb during those two minutes, yet the quarter will have vanished into thin air.

That's merely an annoyance when you're talking about quarters, but I get nervous thinking of Sam with a nine-millimeter handgun. When he's misplaced something, he becomes extremely indignant, as if someone had jumped down out of the sky and taken the item. "Mommy! Someone took my piece! It was here the last time I looked, and now it's gone. Well, it isn't my fault. Can I have another gun, please? I said *please*! C'mon, it's been like a whole three days since I lost the last one!"

Then there is his seeming inability to shut things. It doesn't much matter what it is: a car door, the toilet seat lid, bedroom drawers—he just doesn't possess the closing gene. He claims it's an allergy, but I'm not so sure.

I don't think it's farfetched to expect that the habits my kids exhibit now will be repeated in their actions as adults. Sure, some of the little idiosyncrasies will disappear with maturity, but overall I suspect that the basic proficiencies they exhibit today will simply be redefined as they grow up and pursue their careers.

131

With this in mind, I return to my vision of Sam the police detective...

> As his partner hauls the perpetrator to unsteady feet, the tall blond man bends over and gets within whisper range of the criminal's ear. Talking loudly, he is unrelenting. "Did ya do it? Did ya do it? Did ya do it? Did ya do it? Did ya do it? Did ya? Huh? Did ya?"
>
> It's been a long night, and his partner, Paul, is slightly irritated. To his constant credit, though, he doesn't show it. He and Sam have been partners for more than 10 years, and his patience with him is legendary within their close-knit brotherhood.
>
> Sam is still putting the full-court press on the perp, who is now shaking from the pressure of having this guy in his face. Between stuttering protests of police brutality, he tries to answer the detective's questions, but they're coming too fast for him. "Aren't you gonna confess? C'mon, confess, would ya? C'mon, you know you did it! Aren't you gonna tell us? Are you gonna? Are you gonna? Are you gonna? Are you gonna? Are you gonna? C'mon, you lousy crook, confess already! You did too do it! You know you did! Did too! (Did not) Did too! (Did not) Did too! (Did not) Did too! (Did not) Did too! Did too! Did too!"
>
> Finally, in utter desperation, Paul steps in and cuffs both of them. Nothing is getting accomplished,

he explains, and he really just wants them both to shut up. After all, he's only human. How much can one human being take before he cracks? The bad guy nods excitedly in agreement, and only Paul understands that he's talking about himself.

In the back of the police cruiser, Sam and the criminal continue their bickering as Paul searches desperately for something for his partner to munch on. Like he's always telling his wife, it's amazing how many snacks this guy goes through in a single shift. No matter how much Sam's old lady packs him to eat, he wolfs it all down and is hungry again within minutes. After learning the hard way what his partner is like when hunger strikes, Paul has gotten in the habit of keeping a banana or two handy. Whatever it takes for some peace and quiet. Damn! He's out of everything tonight! All he has is some sugary gum and a half-eaten candy bar, but he's no idiot. He knows what sugar does to Sam.

He sighs and shuts his eyes for a moment, knowing what the ride back to the station will be like. God, he never should have let him have a sip of that soda. It always hypes him up. Sure enough, he hasn't even put the cruiser in gear when Sam starts in on him. "When are we going to be there, Paul? Huh? When? Are we almost there? Geez, it seems like we've been driving for hours!"

The patient man in the driver's seat just rolls his eyes and swallows hard. "Soon enough, Sam" he answers grimly. "Just try to occupy yourself during the ride, okay? We'll be there in about 10 minutes."

Paul turns hopefully to the back. "Hey, if you're good for the whole ride, I'll let you unhook the prisoner with the big key, okay? You liked that last time. Remember how much fun that was, Sammy?"

A small voice from the back answers him. "It wasn't much fun. Besides, you always get to hold the big key. All I ever get is the stupid notebook. The captain likes you more, and you know it!"

Paul massages his aching temples as he drives with one hand. Oh, God, please let him fall asleep for the night. His shift is almost over. Then from the back seat, the voice of his partner once again interrupts his thoughts. "I'm telling the Captain you've been driving with one hand! Na, Na, Na, Na, Na! You're gonna be in big trouble for that one!"

After a quick hearty laugh, Sam gets serious for a second as an idea comes to him. "Hey, I'll make a deal with you. If you let me play with the siren I won't rat you out to the Captain."

Paul just smiles and reaches under his seat. He's just remembered a juice box he hid there earlier. He tosses it into the back seat.

"Hey man!" the prisoner says. "What's the big idea throwing a juice box at me?"

"Sorry, pal. It's for my partner. He gets grouchy when he's hungry."

Sam's slurping prevents any further conversation. Not that it matters; they're at the station now. Paul silently thanks the heavens. Thirty minutes, maybe an hour with the paperwork, then he'll be outta here and in a warm bed with his wife.

Turning to his partner, Paul speaks slowly and clearly. "Now, Sam, listen up. I'm only going in for a minute; I need to get this loser up to Booking. Then I'll be back for you and we'll do the paperwork. I'll let you use the pen if you just sit here quietly and drink your apple juice. Can you do that?"

Sam sniffs, insulted. "I'm 36 years old, Paul. I think I can sit in the back of the police cruiser and wait for you while I drink my apple juice. Whaddya think, I'm some kinda baby or something?"

Two seconds later, the blaring sound of a police siren clears the building. Officers rush the car with weapons drawn. As they get to the cruiser, they stop in disbelief as Sam, grinning widely, sticks his head out of the front seat window.

The rest of the officers file slowly back into the building, jostling each other and laughing at Sam's latest prank. He's well-liked, and they know he's almost always behind the chaos that goes down at the station. But Paul isn't laughing. Furious, he grabs Sam by the jacket and hauls him out of the driver's seat.

"Are you kidding me? I specifically told you not to make any noise, didn't I? Am I going to have to give you a time-out, or do you think you can learn to listen to me the first time?"

Grinning sheepishly, Sam turns on his charm. "Hey, lighten up, will ya? I heard you. But it wasn't me making the noise. It was the siren! And you didn't say anything about the siren making noise, now did you?"

It's amazing what the thought of a child of yours all grown up and no longer needing you can do for your perspective. All of a sudden, I really don't care if he wears a belt tomorrow.

19

Steal My Identity, Slap My Face, and Make Off with My Husband—Please!

SOME WOMEN WON'T ADMIT IT, BUT I WILL: BEING A "STAY-AT-home" mom can lead to a loss of one's mind. One can only hope it's a temporary condition.

It has taken me some time, but I think I've finally figured it out. The reason we feel so overwhelmed much of the time is because the entire universe is against us. No matter what we do, it's never enough. Take the other day, for example. While doing a load of laundry, I bent down and read the little words stamped on the lint trap of the dryer. Do you know what it said? "Clean before loading." Well, fine, then! I climbed the stairs and vacuumed the living room.

Can't anyone, even my clothes dryer, ever be satisfied?

It's like those oval stickers on the backs of nicer cars and SUVs. You've seen them—they announce where the driver has been recently, like "OBX" and "CM." Big deal. I don't even know what all those initials stand for. I'm half tempted to give those braggarts a taste of their own medicine and make up some stickers of my own. I doubt anyone would be able to figure them out. So far, I've come up with "PO" (Principal's Office), "TB" (Taco Bell), and "AFTBG." The last one, an acronym for "Another Friggin' T-Ball Game," is probably too long and bitter for a sticker, but it's catchy.

I'm not yearning to backpack through Europe or anything, but the only times I ever dress up these days is to see someone marry or get buried. That's a little depressing. I haven't stopped growing as a person just because I'm home raising three kids all day. I am still an intelligent, functioning woman who questions life and its meaning. When I see cured meat in the store, I always wonder what was wrong with it before.

Unfortunately, my entertaining is mainly limited to guests who request juice boxes and need to be checked on in the bathroom. This doesn't bother me, for the most part, but what does raise my hackles are magazine articles that offer tips for adult party-givers. The advice the writers offer usually goes something like this:

THREE WEEKS BEFORE PARTY: Handcraft invitations using homemade paper and colored drippings from onions and beets, tie with silk ribbons and calligraphy envelopes.

TWO WEEKS BEFORE PARTY: Mail invitations.

ONE WEEK BEFORE PARTY: Check RSVPs, order fresh flower arrangements from florist.

TWO DAYS BEFORE PARTY: Do all shopping, including alcohol.

DAY BEFORE PARTY: Prepare all desserts, string party lights, check electrical outlets, purchase new music if desired, arrange seating, clean house, set tables, get hair and nails done, and set out outfit for party.

DAY OF PARTY: Make main courses and appetizers, and *enjoy*!

Frankly, I hate anyone organized enough to save one of these lists, much less follow the directions on them. Just getting this list accomplished would leave me with a nervous twitch.

We entertain about once every three to four years. We don't entertain to show off our accomplishments and our possessions, we don't entertain to see our friends and catch up on old times. After schlepping around with the kids and taking care of 17 million things all day long, day in and day out, the last thing I need is a bunch of people critiquing my work. Who needs the pressure? Nope, I entertain for one reason only: to get things done around the house.

Anyone with a busy husband, an old house, and too many kids and dogs to count knows exactly what I'm talking about. Here is *my* appropriate guide to preparing for a party:

139

WEEK BEFORE PARTY: Accidentally break upstairs bathroom window while bending down to clean the toilet in the 5 x 5-foot "master" bathroom.

TWO DAYS BEFORE PARTY: Sprain ankle while running upstairs to see why all three children are screaming hysterically. Introduce yourself to your new tenant, a medium-sized brown bat, who moved in due to the hole in the screen in the upstairs bathroom.

DAY BEFORE PARTY: Realize that the washing machine is leaking, the squirrels have just eaten your new front porch cushions, something smells funky under the sofa and you can't figure out why, and one of the kids practiced spelling "butt" on the living room wall where he or she didn't think anyone would notice.

MORNING OF PARTY: Invite all the neighbors and some old friends to come over tonight for a little get-together at your house, and tell your husband you'll be "entertaining" that evening. Explain to him that this may require him to do some quick home repairs in order for you to avoid embarrassment.

AFTERNOON OF PARTY: Experience severe mood swings, alternating between glares of hatred and a vague mention of divorce from your husband, and extreme giddiness that you are finally getting some things done around the house. Use every carpet cleaner you've ever stocked up on to get the vomit stain out of the middle of the rug, contributed by your youngest daughter who has again eaten twice her body weight in M&M's before remembering why she can't eat chocolate. Suspect your son of having a fever as he uses impeccable manners to ask his sister to get his pillow, and discover you're out of Children's Tylenol. Remind guests not to arrive until after dark, at which time they will be unable to make out all the words you couldn't wash off the living room walls. Dust where anyone may see through the dim lighting. Decide that since you can't get the smell of vomit out of the living room, it's best to light enough scented candles to illuminate Yankee Stadium. Drug the dog, threaten the only child left who isn't sick, and pick up chips and dip. Smile provocatively at your husband as he struggles through a list of household repairs that would realistically take two months to complete, and remind him he has three hours left and still needs to shower.

FIVE MINUTES BEFORE PARTY: Change out of your sweats, hide the laundry under the beds, pay off the kids, check the punch for stray cat hair, realize you don't have enough seating and look in basement for your folding chairs, as your husband reminds you he sold them at your last yard sale for a buck each. Stick "The Best of Raffi" in the CD player because you don't have time to look for grown-up music. *Enjoy*!

It's okay. I'm certain my time will come. There will be a Valentine's Day when I will wear red because I'm seductive, not because my son had a bloody nose. There will be a day when I have time to shave both legs during the same bath.

There will come a time when I will choose a purse because it looks sexy, not because it's large enough to hold several juice boxes and the super-jumbo bargain container of wipes.

If you think you've talked to the dog a little too much this week, I've got a solution. Every now and then, when the monotony becomes overwhelming, I make my own excitement and have a "soap opera day."

It isn't hard to do. I had one yesterday, in fact. First thing in the morning, I swooshed down the stairs, surprising Mike, who was putting on his work boots. "Heels and a scarf at seven A.M.? Are you okay?" I flashed a sexy smile and tossed my head. "Of course, Stryker," I purred. "I'm going to prepare breakfast."

He felt my forehead. "You don't look sick. Why are you talking weird and calling me Stryker? And what bit you on the cheek?"

Sighing deeply, I leaned into him. "Listen, I'm having a soap opera day to try to glam up my life a little, so if you wouldn't give me a hard time I'd appreciate it. Nobody is ever named Mike, so I renamed you for the day. And that's not a bug bite on my cheek, it's a fake mole. All the soap stars have them."

Shaking his head, Stryker left for work.

He obviously didn't understand my need for a crazy girlfriend to steal my identity, slap my face, and make off with my husband. Just for one day, it would be neat if someone I thought was dead and buried surprised me with a knock at the door. The camera would pan in on my shocked face as my long nails stretched dramatically over my mouth, open in awe.

Mothers whose jewelry is dried macaroni and not diamonds need days like this. If you follow my advice, the next time one of your kids throws a temper tantrum in the middle of the supermarket, you can say to yourself, "Well, at least I can be thankful that it's not my evil identical twin trying to poison me!"

I don't watch soap operas, but I've seen the commercials. I know old Wawa coffee cups and school papers never fall out of the car door when opened by soap stars. These women never clean toilets or have hair that blows in the wind. Their breath is minty fresh, their teeth large and gleaming. They have background music instead of barking dogs and kids begging them to spell "diarrhea." They wear tops that reveal their décolletage. They use words like "décolletage."

Occasionally my soap opera day doesn't work out all that well. Once I poured the kids' breakfast juice into margarita glasses and rolled their silverware up in paper napkins (the whole effect was more "Denny's" than "Spago," but I liked it). Then Sam, who I'd renamed "Link" for the day, spilled his juice. As his head whipped up, I anticipated a yell and smiled. "Ah, the spirit of youth." Scared, Link ran from the kitchen. He must not have known that soap stars always appear to be in control, unless of course they're playing the part of the deranged loser.

That day, I was playing the part of the patient, loving mother who never gets mad at her children.

A few hours later, I was worn out. Cleaning in heels is always exhausting, and my fake mole had run and merged with my lipstick, scaring the dogs. By the time Stryker stopped home for lunch I had abandoned the whole idea.

"How'd it work out today, babe?" he wanted to know. "Did anyone get amnesia? Did you foil any evil plots to freeze the town?" I looked at him wistfully, still half-expecting the faint sounds of background music to pipe in. "Nah. Anyway, without six last names, I'm way out of my league. I'm back to my normal old self again."

Smiling, he left the room. Stryker was way too smart to respond to that.

20

Boy Feet

THE MONELL RESEARCH CENTER IN PHILADELPHIA WAS RECENTLY given the job to develop the ultimate stink bomb. Apparently, our government needs to develop a smell so repulsive as to be considered unbearable by people from all cultures.

During military testing, volunteers wore hoods while the offensive odors were slowly infused. At the first sign of effectiveness, the volunteers' heads jerked back, their faces contorted with revulsion. While trying to inhale as little of the smell as possible, test subjects suffer increased heart rate and queasiness.

As a mother of a little boy, I have felt their pain. Actually, I think our country should enlist the help of mothers in their search for the ultimate weapon.

One has rarely encountered a stench so vile as that of a lunchbox baked in 90-degree heat in the trunk over summer vacation, containing a decaying peach, rancid yogurt, and the remains of a tuna sandwich. The mere threat of such an offensive odor could end war as we know it.

And if that combination doesn't obliterate the olfactory powers of the enemy, one could simply follow up the attack with boy feet. This phenomenon is closely related to man feet, the power of which in the field of offensiveness needs no advertising. This is a year-round assault on the senses, especially if the boy just wore sneakers with no socks.

There have already been countless victims of boy feet, including thousands of innocent mothers who naively drove home from a pleasant afternoon in the park, only to stop the car for fear they had somehow gotten tangled up in the carcass of a rotting skunk.

Mother (slamming on the brakes) "Oh no! Have I just run over a skunk?" Gasping for air, she turns, warning her kids to stay put. Cautiously opening her door, she places her feet square on the pavement and peers underneath the car. Hmm. Nothing.

Confused, she looks around. No trash dumpster nearby, no landfill, no sewage pipe emptying into the street before her, no billowing smokestack of rancid pollution. There wasn't so much as a stray cigarette discarded by the curbside. Nothing. Yet the smell had been something otherworldly, almost inhuman in nature.

Unwilling to surrender her search, she checks the bumper and the tread of each tire. Nothing.

Shrugging her shoulders, she opens her door once again and starts to smile at her kids, waiting patiently for her in the back seat.

So is the smell.

In a shot, she realizes the source of the stench.

The sweet-faced little boy in the rear had simply popped off his sneakers and rested his feet on the driver's seat.

Here are several other smells that should be registered as lethal weapons:

1. The moldy raw potato decorated in Sunday School last year, kept in a shoebox in your daughter's closet, which she can't even discuss throwing away without bursting into tears.

2. The inside of your husband's tackle box with at least one lure still attached to a tiny bit of what you hope is bait. Either way, it puts you off sushi for life.

3. The infamous open-toed sandals, bought in May, smelled in late August, belonging to your son and worn anyplace where there was moisture.

4. The Tupperware container your husband found underneath the front seat of his truck, which he

kindly placed in the kitchen sink for you to clean. It holds a banana peel and half a chicken salad sandwich. You haven't made chicken salad since last October.

5. The "yogurt experiment" that the kids started in the basement and then forgot about.

6. Your daughter's softball team socks that her coach needs back for next season, which starts in a week. Miraculously standing by their own power, they are found upright in the back of her closet. They appear to be mocking you, daring you to touch them. The dog, who followed you into the closet, runs away whimpering as you finally knock them to the ground with a broom.

If it seems as if most of these smells are of distinctly male origin, well, I just report the facts as I smell them. If you have any odiferous items lying around your house that could help your country in a time of war, by all means, let the government know. Just don't send them to me. I've got my own problems.

21

I May Not Remember Your Name, but I Know I Gave Birth to You

I WAS DUSTING, WHICH ALWAYS PUTS ME IN A BAD MOOD anyway, when I saw it. A tiny, albino mouse who had apparently curled up to take his last breath in one of my Wedgwood teacups. I dropped it, of course, and it broke— the teacup, that is, not the mouse.

It was then that I realized it wasn't a dead albino mouse at all, but a clump of fine blond baby hair from my son, the remnants of his very first haircut seven years earlier.

I know what you're probably thinking. What kind of a mother would store her kid's baby hair in a teacup?

Oh, sure, I started out like you. I swore I'd be different. I'd save every drawing, tying them up in bundles with pale pink or blue satin ribbons. I'd record the first time they ate an ice cream cone, know which kid hated raisins, and never forget how old they were when they took their first steps. Ultimately, I realized that this kind of thinking will get you nowhere.

Obviously, I seriously underestimated the work involved in keeping my children's baby books up-to-date. Now I understand why mine, dug out of a box in my parents' attic, was never used. I used to think it was because I was totally unloved as a child, but as my mother reminded me, I was the youngest. I never knew what that really meant, figuring I was lucky to get fed, but now I know.

Before I had kids of my own, though, I was a bit put off by how little my parents bothered with the details of my birth. It's almost as if someone dropped me in my crib and they turned their heads to murmur how cute I was, then went back to reading the newspaper. There are no cute recordings of baby babble and no baggie filled with clippings from my first haircut.

They didn't even give me a middle name.

I can picture the discussion on that topic. "Don, you know I've had another girl. This makes, oh, I don't know, three? Anyway, since it needs a name, could you at least suggest the middle one?"

My father, ensconced in the only comfortable chair in the house, pauses to glance down over the top of his paper. "Well, I don't feel like giving it a middle name. Why don't you just cut bangs on it like the others so we know it's ours?"

These are the same people who didn't bother to give me a Godparent.

I understand they were busy. I know that because, in the baby book, under "weight," they scribbled "busy." Other than that one word and a newspaper clipping about my arrival, not cut but ripped out of the local paper, the book is empty.

"Haircolor." Blank.

"Eyes." Blank.

"Parents." Blank.

You get the picture.

So, naturally, I vowed that the minute my first baby came home from the hospital I would set about recording every adorable move he or she made.

The first year, I did really well. In fact, all three baby books are bursting with fun facts and pertinent information. Looking back, I see I even found the time to write down every single bowel movement my twins had for the first three weeks they were home. That's just sick.

But around age two, and definitely by the third child, my recollections start drifting off a bit. I felt really bad about this recently, on Dylan's kindergarten graduation day.

The afternoon before, her teacher sent home a note asking that parents bring in the child's baby book for graduation. As a surprise to the students, each parent could stand up and read an excerpt of a meaningful memory from the book.

My daughter's teacher was 25 and had no kids. I doubt she even had a houseplant. I had never known her to have a cruel streak, but there was something sadistic about the assignment, in my opinion.

That night, I skimmed through the entries in my daughter's anemic thin volume. She'd been the last baby, so I'm sure it wouldn't be too hard to find something touching that we'd recorded. Right?

Wrong.

It was glaringly apparent that I'd need to be *very* creative at graduation the next morning.

Sure enough, at graduation I listened to other parents eloquently recall their fondest memories of Josh, Jake, Amanda, and Emily. Then it was my turn. I knew I could pass with a simple wave of the hand, and remain seated, giving up my turn to the next parent on the evil list.

Sure. And be branded for life as the loser parent who couldn't recall anything wonderful about her own kid. There was more judging going on in that room than on the last day of the OJ trial.

Clearing my throat, I took the stage.

I smiled at the audience, winking at Dylan in the first row. Turning to a page that, in reality, possessed nothing more than an unmarked photograph of our family on the boardwalk, I began to read.

"Today Dylan and I spent our first day at the park. We fed the pigeons, and I marveled at the joy in her face as she watched them eat the bread we brought. The day was shining and bright, but it paled in comparison to the sunshine in my heart as I fell in love all over again with my beautiful baby girl."

I took a deep breath. I suspected there was someone reaching for a tissue in the audience, but I didn't want to jinx myself by looking. "On the way home, Dylan said her first word, 'birdie,' and my heart leapt with joy. Oh, what is love? I say it is the smile of a baby, her smell; her very essence. Today, witnessed only by some pigeons and a little girl in a stroller, I discovered the meaning of love."

With a deep sigh, I closed the book and made my way back to my seat, but not before I saw at least five people reaching in their handbags for tissues. Aha! Got 'em!

I may be a rotten mother, but at least I could write.

Of course, the guilt set in later, especially after Dylan insisted on holding the book on the way home. It took approximately 3.5 minutes for her to figure out that there was no page like the one I had read in her book.

It took approximately two Happy Meals and one expensive trip to Toys "R" Us for her to forgive me.

Recently, I got a roll of film developed that had been left in our camera for an unknown period of time. The pictures were of the same child taking her first steps *and* going on a class trip to Storybook Land. I don't know why this surprised me: the framed photos scattered about our house all show smiling babies with mostly gums showing.

153

During every pregnancy, I assumed I'd be one of those hyper-organized mothers. I bought expensive baby books and huge scrapbooks that just itched to be filled with cherished mementos. Somewhere along the line though, I was outnumbered.

Now that the kids are getting older, it isn't just my organizational skills that are waning—my memory is going, too. I've come up with little tricks though. For example, I've found that people look at you oddly if, while yelling at one of your kids, you mistakenly call him by the dog's name. To avoid this, I merely point to the offender while saying, "Don't make me come over there!" It's direct, it's effective and, most importantly, I don't have to get the name right.

One must understand that there are side effects to frequent and unabated mothering. The minute I became outnumbered by children, I started down that long path forged by mothers who came before me. If a shoelace dangles, we tie it. If a zipper hangs low, we zip it. Our heads spin around when we hear "Mom!" even if it's another kid calling another mother.

We provide the spit for the dirty faces who appear before us. If a hand opens up, we hold it. We cut the meat, butter the bread, and hand over our change. It's our job.

And, like any job, it takes a toll. I fed a kid lunch the other day and he wasn't even mine. In my defense, he was on the front porch and he did look vaguely familiar. But I think he should have told me he was merely a small-boned Jehovah's

Witness before he ate the last brownie. In retrospect, his briefcase should have tipped me off, but I thought it was some fancy computer game.

Waving goodbye to him, I thought it was a shame he wasn't one of mine. He was such a good eater.

22

Open Season
on Glue Gun Users

No One Understands, Until They Have Three Kids In School, how many cute things they bring home that you just have to save. I'm not talking about report cards or school pictures—they always get shoved in a drawer because they come in envelopes.

I'm talking about the macaroni Jesus they made in Vacation Bible School at age four. I'm talking about the handprints your son made you on Mother's Day at age three that stained his hands for two weeks and ruined his bedroom carpet, but which he and his father did as a surprise for you, reducing you to tears.

The first tooth your youngest daughter lost that made you cry because you knew no baby of yours would ever lose a first tooth again. She was the last, and it meant so much more. The mangled, dried-up dandelion that your oldest daughter saved from the cemetery of the funeral you weren't sure if she should attend, but let her because it was her beloved grandmother. The first baseball mitt your son ever wore, tiny now even against his hand. The dog-eared program from your girls' first ever ballet recital when they forgot all the moves and stood on stage and just smiled from ear to ear. The tiny piece of paper you found shoved in your daughter's underwear drawer with a backward phone number of her new best friend in kindergarten.

These aren't mementos, really. They're life in its most physical form, and you just cannot dispose of any of it.

But where do you put it all? If you're like me, you shove it on top of your desk and straighten the pile every now and then when it starts to lean to one side.

When you are allergic to crafts and have no idea how to do any of it, you dread things like organizing all of your kids' stuff. This may come easy to other women, but not to me. Still, when my pile of keepsakes and cherished paperwork started spilling off the desk, I knew I had to do something.

When you don't know *how* to do something, you should go to the source. So I started reading the circulars that come in the mail from all those gigantic craft warehouses. Usually, I toss them right in the trash—after all, who needs that kind of pressure and self-loathing?

I don't wear an apron and have no idea what a topiary is. Does that make me a bad person?

If you are one of those women who can tie a balloon without using a toe, and if you can work yourself up into a froth over the thought of collecting acorns for a homemade centerpiece at Thanksgiving, you won't relate. (It's not your fault; you just got some different genetic markers than I did.) But if you're like me, you'll know what I mean when I say I was out in the hall when God handed out the glue gun gene.

Why do these women in the magazines and circulars look so darn happy—like they've just won something? I'll tell you right now that if someone told me I'd have to knit a cozy for my toaster I'd pour myself a big glass of wine. No one would want to use my scowling face on the cover of a craft magazine, that's for certain.

But these women are different. They always appear in an apron that says something cutesy, like "#1 MOM." If they're already good at crafts, why do they have to flaunt it? You don't see me prancing around in an apron that says, "Sucks At Making Pretty Things But Throws A Mean Fastball."

These women have broad grins that show off really large white teeth. The image is not complete, however, without the requisite blonde children at their feet, usually two, who are always spotlessly clean with matching white smiles. The kids never look like they would if they were helping *me* with a craft. My kids would be cowering in a corner somewhere, holding their ears against a barrage of curses.

I can understand being crafty if you have no choice in the matter. For example, if one happens to live on a remote farm, it makes sense for one to can her own fruit, make her own decorations, and sew her own clothing.

But why, why, why, oh Lord, would anyone, without a glue gun being held to her head, want to make something she could easily go pick up at Wal-Mart? These women make things like candles, and wreaths, and homemade wrapping paper. Do they not understand that these items don't cost all that much and you can buy them almost anywhere?

And they look so happy! The photos show them, with such purpose and joy, putting together intricate gingerbread houses and wreaths for the front door for the holidays. All the expected weapons are there, in plentiful supply. They have glue guns of every shape and size, boxes of glitter, and whole rooms devoted to putting this stuff together.

That's another problem I have. Maybe if I had a whole room set aside in which I could experiment and develop my abilities, I wouldn't be such a loser—but no, whenever I have something I need to assemble, there I am at the kitchen table, pushing the bills to one side, wiping up the crumbs, and working in a two-inch area of free space. Is it any wonder I'm not smiling?

You know what? I don't think the women and children in these circulars and magazines are normal. There are some clues that lead me to believe they're faking it—like the fact that not one kid is trying to wrench a pinecone out of the hand of another; no one is aiming the glue gun at her sister's head, and the dog isn't in the corner eating some fake

160

greenery that will later force mom and dad to put the house up for sale.

If you don't have the natural ability, or even the desire, to do this kind of stuff, then you shouldn't even try. But there have been times when I just couldn't help myself—I had to dip my toe into their world. It's never worked, and the attempts have left me broke and defeated.

Take, for example, the time I decided to organize my children's most cherished memorabilia. I was going to put together a loving, beautiful "memory book" for each child. The first thing I needed to do was visit a place that, previously, I had driven past with the same sense of wonderment one would have on a tour of Alcatraz.

What kind of secrets lie inside and who dares to enter?

I'm speaking of a craft warehouse. We're talking about a veritable palace of glue guns, crepe paper, and special scissors that some people actually go to *on purpose*. It's like Disney World to them. I've been told there are armed guards outside some of these places who are prepared to shoot you on sight if you can't use the expression "scrap-booking" in a sentence. And it's not even a real word!

Anyway, I dug a cute little sweatshirt out of the bottom of my dresser and put my hair in a ponytail in order to blend in. After all, if I was going to do it, the least I could do was look the part. I made it through the entrance without getting shot, but immediately realized I couldn't fake it—I was sure to be recognized as an alien intruder. Walking down that

161

first aisle took me right back to the time I accidentally entered the men's room at a Phillies game.

The women I encountered in these aisles were *good*. They knew the difference between regular and puffy paint. They didn't browse with their jaws hanging open down row after row of tiny containers filled with plastic baby bottles, miniature umbrellas, and the like. I had no idea what these things were used for. Who uses a baby bottle the size of a thumbnail? I overheard one woman tell another she was making individual baby shower favors for her friend. I made a mental note to invite her to my next party. She was not only crafty, she was doing it because she *enjoyed* it! I had no idea they made so many women like this and, frankly, I was awestruck.

Unfortunately, I made the mistake of asking a sales clerk if I needed a permit to buy a glue gun. Although she tried not to laugh, several other people in the aisle did, and one little girl pointed at me as her mother whispered something in her ear. As much as I had tried to hide my deficiencies, they were as obvious as a third leg. I slunk down the next aisle and tried to keep my questions to myself, but it was hopeless. The truth was out.

I wasn't a true crafter. I don't stare at my utility meter as I think of creative ways to conceal it with a festive box. Frankly, I don't get the whole "concealing" thing anyway. If you don't want it to appear that there's a toaster on your counter, why would you want some pink-and-purple knitted oblong thing? Is that supposed to look more natural than a naked toaster? The only thing out of place in my kitchen is Mike. Somehow, I doubt he'd appreciate it if I covered him with a colorful cozy.

By the time I got to the checkout line I'd spent a small fortune. Apparently, you cannot put together a memory book without special scissors that make little ocean patterns when you cut. You also need borders of every shape, size, and color, and clever stickers that say things like, "Uh Oh, Someone Forgot To Smile!" so you can jazz up each photo. I was about ready to paste that one on my forehead.

In retrospect, for the money I ended up spending I could have had Cindy Crawford paste my children's mementos to her body and parade around the house. Or, for even less money, I could have simply built an addition on the back of the house to keep all their stuff in.

You may ask yourself, what would a gal like me do with all of that memory book stuff once she got it home? Would she instinctively know what to do with it? Or would she panic and realize she had just spent her children's' college money on three lousy books?

It took me two months. I sat down several nights a week at my kitchen table, agonized over which colored markers to use and which stickers to apply, and put together a memory book for my oldest. I had no time for television, reading to my children, or discussing current affairs with my husband.

My sex life suffered and I began to grind my teeth in my sleep.

On the other hand, it cleared up one-third of the clutter and alleviated some of my parental guilt.

In the end, I was happy with my foray into the world of crafts. I was no better at it, having proved incorrect the theory that "practice makes perfect." I learned why people become obsessed with their crafts, because you can't do it "a little." That's like "sort of" knowing how to swim.

Plus, doing things I don't like leads to irritability, not perfection. Unfortunately, I still had two more books to put together. My refusal to make even one more ocean wave cutout with my fancy new scissors had given me a real attitude problem. I'd developed an allergic reaction to pasting things together. My body was rebelling.

Suddenly, I felt a kinship with my parents, who had realized 30-some years ago that by the time you get to the last couple of kids you've got to make sacrifices. I had a tough choice to make—my sanity or an organized lifestyle.

I wimped out, of course, and was rescued by my Mike, who by then had started to notice the teeth grinding and the waning sex life. He didn't care if he had a wife who could stitch him a new wallet. He didn't care if he had a wife who cut regular, straight, ordinary lines instead of fancy wavy lines with her scissors. He was okay if I went back to the old me. The woman who had time to shave her legs, comb her hair, and take more pictures that would have nowhere to go.

So, overwhelmed by a mountain of costly organizational supplies I had no room for, I quietly asked Mike to solve the problem.

True to form, he never once made me feel bad. He didn't insist on buying me a new apron with "#1 Failure" scrolled across the front. He didn't mentally add up how much money I had wasted. And he never once said, "I told you so."

He simply went to one of those other stores—you know, one of those huge home improvement warehouses where men like to congregate—and spent $21 for three big crates. He borrowed one of my fancy markers and wrote a child's name on each of them. He didn't even berate himself for not writing the names in calligraphy.

We had them filled in less than 10 minutes.

While he worked, he wore a white construction belt with big pockets in the front. At first glance, it resembled an apron. The kids were thrilled that their things were organized, and they smiled up at him as he heaved the containers onto a shelf. He was laughing; they were laughing.

I looked at the picture of the woman on the circular. I looked back at Mike and cocked my head. The dog was in the corner, sleeping peacefully. My husband's teeth, the kids' teeth—heck, even the dog's teeth were gleaming in the afternoon sun. I glanced back at the circular.

It was hard to believe. Sure, I had to overlook the broad shoulders, but if I squinted my eyes and blurred my vision just so, it was the same scene!

23

A.K.A. Julie McCoy, Cruise Director Extraordinaire

A LOT OF BUSY MOMS I KNOW TEND TO LUMP TOGETHER THE stuff they don't get to all year long and say, "Oversummer-vacationI'llgettoit."

I hope they make out better with that plan than I do, 'cause over my kids' summer vacation I never get to 99 percent of the things I think I'll get to. You know why? Because if school ends at 1:00 P.M. on the 15th of June, at 1:01 P.M. on the 15th of June I turn into Julie McCoy.

You remember Julie McCoy, don't you?—the perky cruise director on *The Love Boat*? Although I'm missing the fancy title, respect, and smart little uniform she wore, and there's no theme music or laugh track, I'm her. For some reason, and I think it may be a universal mother thing, I become The Person Who Must Organize Everything And Who Is Also,

By The Way, In Charge Of Information About Things Big And Small.

My husband, who is out among the living each and every day, will inevitably come home from work and ask me, an individual trapped at home all day with three kids, what the weather is supposed to be like tomorrow. As a matter of fact, if we lived in the Midwest I'd be the one everyone would turn to if a funnel cloud appeared outside our window. They'd immediately want to know why I'd failed to warn them.

Once in our underground shelter, I'd have to whip up dinner so no one turned on anyone else in a grumpy fit. Since that's where the washer and dryer are located, I'd be asked if there were any clean jeans, and if I knew where the television remote was. Again, note that we would be hiding at that particular time, in a basement shelter, awaiting the imminent arrival of a killer tornado.

It doesn't matter. I am still The Person Who Must Organize Everything And Who Is Also, By The Way, In Charge Of Information About Things Big And Small. Don't forget that.

Any conversation that would take place would go something like this: "Hey, honey? Did you happen to throw any whites in this afternoon? Because I don't like the way these socks bunch up. If a tornado is coming I should really be able to run in my good socks with the elastic still intact."

My son, meanwhile, turning away from the window with a frightened glare, would accuse me of failing the family. "What happened? When you got our clothes out this morning you didn't tell us to dress for a *tornado*!"

I stammer, feeling slightly guilty for some reason. "I'm sorry, everyone. I watched CNN and The Weather Channel, and downloaded the local forecast like always. This must be a rogue cell that developed somewhere along the Mississippi and caught me by surprise. It will never happen again, I promise!"

Interrupted by a long, dramatic sigh, I would then immediately turn to Dylan. "Yes, sweetie?" "Well, mom, with a twister out there, how are McKenna and I supposed to get to ballet?" I'd reassure her, trying not to notice the hail pounding at the basement windows. "Don't worry, honey, I'll get you to ballet. After all, I hand-washed your tights and scratched your initials in your new dance shoes with my bare nail until it was bloody and raw." Satisfied, she'd turn back to watching the impending doom. "Good."

Suddenly, McKenna would burst into tears, grabbing me tight. Thinking that she's just scared of the storm, I'd attempt to calm her. "It'll be all right, darling. Don't worry."

Wiping tears from her eyes, she'd look up at me. "It's not that, mommy! I don't have Lion! I have to have Lion! How could you forget to bring my favorite stuffed animal when we were rushing to the basement?"

169

Rubbing her shoulders and feeling like a terrible mother, I'd apologize. "I'm so sorry, sweetie. My hands were full with the wedding pictures, the pets, and flashlights. I'll make another trip upstairs as soon as I finish braiding your hair."

Noticing the loud gurgling to my left, I'd wearily turn back to my husband. "What's that noise?"

Smiling weakly and rubbing his belly, he'd answer wanly. "Oh, nothing, just my stomach. I didn't eat all day. I could really go for something like a casserole. Is there anything to nibble on down here?"

I'd look around the darkened basement, wind whipping leaves and branches up against the rattling windows. All I'd see were some old lawn chairs, lots of storage crates, the washer/dryer combo, and an entire cobwebbed area that I'd successfully avoided for the last five years.

"No, darling, but I'll risk my life to climb up into the kitchen and whip up a quick tuna casserole for everyone."

Moans would suddenly erupt from all three children. "Tuna casserole? We hate tuna casserole! We want pizza!" I'd sigh, rubbing the nervous twitch over my right eye and praying the roof would blow off soon.

"Well, I guess it's possible, if I run fast and stay close to the ground, that I could make it to the car without getting swept up in a violent funnel cloud, if it's still in our drive-way, that is. And I might be able to successfully navigate my way through the dangerous streets to locate a town not devastated by the twister and locate someone, anyone who is still working through this mayhem. If I could do that, I could probably manage to pick up a pizza." I'd let out a long sigh for drama. "Of course, it would probably be cold by the time I got back."

"That's okay, mommy! We *love* cold pizza!"

As the laugh track bursts forth with programmed hilarity, I'd turn and face my family, hand on hip, and flash a wry grin. I've never used a wry grin, but I think it's about time I did. Besides, it's very big in the sitcom world. Instead of getting frustrated—another biggie in my house but not so much in the sitcom world—I'd shake my head and say something witty that was thought up by eight underpaid writers at a table. Something like, "And I love *you*!"

As the laugh track bursts forth one last time, the credits roll and we fade to a commercial.

Brought to you in living color by neighborhood mothers everywhere.

24

It's All Good

IT'S NOT THAT I DON'T LOVE THE MULTIFACETED CAREER I HAVE chosen—I do. But if management could delegate a few jobs here and there, I'd be able to spend a little more time working on my book and less time trying to get the bare minimum accomplished around the house.

The problem is that my kids are like pint-sized union bosses, each and every one of them. It started when they got hold of my husband's union by-laws. They read it together one night before bed while I was taking a shower. They helped each other with the difficult words and before I knew it, they were starting to scare me.

"I cannot possibly make my bed right now. I have just put my shoes away, and according to Section 8, paragraph 2b, I require a 20-minute break. I'd love a juice box and a snack, please!"

I tried paying them off, but it got too expensive. "Sorry, mom, but two bucks to sweep the front porch and pick up all the toys on the lawn? That's not even close to the going rate. For my level of expertise I should be getting five bucks for that, plus another two-fifty contributed to my vacation fund."

It's not like I'm trying to get the kids to do these chores for *me*. All mothers know it's for their own good. We want them to develop a good work ethic and realize that a family that works together, works. Or something like that. Unfortunately, my kids are not much help.

One time I was really pleased that my son spent an entire hour washing the windows. He looked like he was putting a serious effort into the job. The only problem is, he used saliva. Somewhere, it seems, he had heard the phrase "spit and polish" and taken it to heart.

When summer vacation arrives, mothers automatically understand that their workload triples, plus they have lost any free time they scrounged up during the school year to get anything important accomplished.

What amazes me the most is the advice parenting manuals give to mothers like me. I eagerly search them out during the month of May, just so I'll be prepared once school is out.

"Put them in the tub," one article said. "Give them some toys to play with, or some shaving cream to express their creativity, and they will keep busy for hours."

Yeah, right! Hard porcelain, slippery floors, three children of mixed gender, and some shaving cream. Can you count the minutes until I'm racing to the emergency room?

Then there's always the innocuous advice to "let them cook. This will foster their abilities in the kitchen while saving you valuable time." Could these people possibly have children of their own?

The only interest my children have in the kitchen is to stand in front of an open refrigerator as they stare down 37 boxes of juice. "Moooooommmm! I can't find any juice boxes!" Of course, at the time I've been in the shower for 10 minutes and they've held the door open so long their nostril hair is getting frosty.

Sometimes I approach summer vacation with the vigor of an explorer to a new land. At times like this, with the lyrics to "Cat's in the Cradle" running through my mind, I remember that they're only young once. That's when I start my list of things I've always wanted to do as a parent.

These are activities that are always better in theory than they are in practice. Perpetrated by well-meaning magazine features that picture model moms and kids being paid to smile, they don't work as well when the kids aren't being paid.

Still, in early June, with these images fresh in my head, I'm willing to seek out new parks and even to drive a little farther than usual. I envision lazy nights spent chasing fireflies and eating ice cream. After all, at least I won't be freaking out at 7:30 in the morning, worrying about finding a missing shoe so we won't be late for school. I won't have to wrestle stray mittens from the dog's mouth, or shuck a lazy child from a warm bed. Nope. No pressure in the summer at all. Just lazy days and endless nights of fun, fun, fun.

By mid-June, I'm stocking the kitchen with refreshing snacks and thinking of the great parties we could host. I make vague plans with other neighborhood moms to take educational trips with the kids in July and August when the boredom sets in. I dust off the beach chairs, trim the girls' hair, and buy a book about making perfume out of garden flowers.

By the end of June, I've been sapped of my patience and the kids have only been out of school for a little over a week. Worse yet, I've realized that all they really want to do is:

1. Bicker from 8:45 A.M. until roughly 8:55 P.M.

2. Discuss, in depth, 7,238 times, who is staring at whom and why whoever is staring at whomever is gonna get it.

176

3. Discuss, in depth, 7,238 times the exact definition of what it means to "get it."

4. Use the words "fart," "burp," "poop," "jerk," and "booger" 609 times, plus variations such as "pain in the butt" and/or "booger butt."

5. Kick each other under the table, even after being separated and defying the laws of physics by somehow continuing to reach one another's shins from opposite ends of the table.

6. Call their bestest friend in the whole wide world and wait for 38 minutes on hold as their friend puts the phone down to finish watching the SpongeBob Squarepants Marathon on Nickelodeon.

7. Use all 28 glasses in the house, including the ones mommy keeps in the good china cabinet, in a four-hour period, to take approximately one-and-a-half sips of water.

8. Use the $8 wedge of Brie for one sandwich before realizing it's not marshmallow spread and throwing it in the sink in disgust.

This is usually when I sit my kids down and have one of my talks with them. I start off thinking it will be just like when the Bradys or the Cosbys had one of their family meetings.

"Okay, listen up. This summer is getting off on the wrong foot, and I'm putting a stop to it right now. We will view this as a learning experience and go on. When momma shakes from fury, that's the sign to stop doing whatever it is you are currently doing."

"Management has deemed it unacceptable to use mommy and daddy's spare checks as drawing paper. You will no longer feed the extra bean burrito on 'Mexican Night' to the dog; we all pay for it later. You do not need to prove a sign wrong when it says, 'Wet Paint.' The refrigerator is not an air-conditioner to stand in front of for 30 minutes while I shower each afternoon. We will no longer tolerate any of you interrupting church services to report what daddy says when he hits his thumb with a hammer. And, finally, there will be no more dragging your little sister's head across the rug to see her hair stand on end from static electricity. I can't get a comb through it as it is. Do we understand each other?"

I sigh, watching three sets of eyes blinking at me. Well, at least they listened.

"Can we go play now?"

They look pretty cute, freckled already from the sun, bare legs hanging over the edge of the sofa. "Yeah, go play."

On their way out the door, one of them accidentally lets the cat out, another trips and falls, and the third one spies the ice cream man turning the corner. I grab my pocketbook, toss the cat inside, and help the whimpering kid to her feet.

Somehow, I already know it's going to be a hectic summer. I'm pretty sure they'll never stop bickering. There will be some days when I'm working at my computer and, simultaneously, one kid will plop on my lap with crayons, another will bleed for no reason, and a third will need something wiped. My only hope of getting some work done between June and September may be to escape into the uppermost branches of the tallest tree in the yard.

On the other hand, I know there will be lazy nights on the porch watching them stall as long as possible in order to suck every last ounce of joy from the day. There will be sleepy afternoons in the backseat as we drive home from a fun day at the beach. There will be stories written that, years from now, will be the memories of one summer when they were six and seven years old.

One summer that will only happen once.

How lucky am I to be part of this magic?

"C'mon, let's get some ice cream. For some reason, I feel like celebrating!"

Hooting and hollering, they take off running barefoot across a lawn that needs mowing to flag down the speeding ice cream man. There's laundry and dust piling up inside, my manuscript sits like a neon beacon on my desk, and there are 30 other things I have to do before dinnertime.

179

Maybe I won't get my book done this month. Maybe I will, and it will be great. Or it won't be, and my only claim to fame will be the three children currently standing before me.

And that's probably the very best part of being a mother.

Because no matter what, I've already got everything I ever wanted. If the only thing I accomplish out of my day is spending some time licking drippy ice cream cones with three happy little kids, then I've achieved something. And I'm happy with that.

About the Author

Melissa Jarvis's humor column, "Family Album," appears weekly in *The Courier-Post* (http://www.courierpostonline.com) and occasionally in other Gannett newspapers.

Melissa is a natural writer who is quite content with her lack of formal education. When she realized at a young age that her parents forgot to give her a middle name, she knew she'd never get anywhere as a scholar. Thankfully, this left her time to sit around and observe the absurdities of life.

She lectures each evening to a bored crowd at the dinner table who pretend to listen as they pour salad dressing over everything on their plates.

Far from a paragon of motherly perfection, she freely admits to taping her daughters' hems. She does, however, take great pride in her boogie boarding skills, not to mention her wicked fastball and killer cheesecake.

Melissa lives in South Jersey with her husband, three children, and assorted pets. *Welcome to the Motherhood* is her first book. She may be reached at MJWritestuff@aol.com.